SOURCEBOOK OF CONTEMPORARY ARCHITECTURE

Sourcebook of
Contemporary Architecture

Àlex Sánchez Vidiella

HARPER
DESIGN
An Imprint of Harper Collins Publishers

SOURCEBOOK OF CONTEMPORARY ARCHITECTURE
Copyright © 2011 by **HARPER DESIGN** and **LOFT Publications**

HarperCollins books may be purchased for educational, business, or sales promotional use. For information, please write: Special Markets Department, HarperCollins*Publishers*, 10 East 53rd Street, New York, NY 10022.

First published in a larger edition in 2007 by:
Harper Design
An Imprint of HarperCollins*Publishers*
10 East 53rd Street
New York, NY 10022
Tel.: (212) 207-7000
Fax: (212) 207-7654
harperdesign@harpercollins.com
www.harpercollins.com

Distributed throughout the world by:
HarperCollins*Publishers*
10 East 53rdStreet
New York, NY 10022
Fax: (212) 207-7654

Editorial coordinator: Catherine Collin
Assistant to editorial coordination: Claire Dalquié, Pilar González Aragón, Sandra Moya, Lou Andrea Savoir
Editor and text: Àlex Sánchez Vidiella
Translation: Cillero & De Motta, Jay Noden
Art director: Mireia Casanovas Soley
Layout: Zahira Rodríguez Mediavilla
Cover layout: Maria Eugenia Castell Carballo

Cover photo: © Brígida González, Christian Richters
Back cover photo: © Bitter Bredt

Library of Congress Control Number: 2010928178

ISBN: 978-0-06-208369-2

Printed in Spain

INTRODUCTION

The world has become a global stage. In modern times, news spreads rapidly all over the planet when events occur in even the remotest areas, or when buildings are constructed, regardless of location. This global condition has come about with the unification of architecture the world over, in which there is now only one tradition: modernity.

Throughout the ages, traditions in different regions of the world have been markedly different. A Mayan palace in Central America, for example, was entirely different from a Romanesque palace in Central Europe, a Moorish palace in the Middle East, or a Chinese palace in the Far East. Things could not have been otherwise. However, this is no longer so. In the world today, the same skyscraper may be found in Mexico City, London, Dubai, or Tokyo, and nobody would give it a second thought. It might even be designed by the same architect.

Of course, this does not rule out exceptions which, by their very nature, are more noticeable. An obvious example of this is the way C.Y. Lee and Partners (Taipei, Taiwan) have explored inspiration from traditional Chinese architecture that is embodied in the Taipei 101 Tower through a set of inverted square pyramid bases, placed one on top of the other, thereby segmenting the building's verticality. The resulting jagged salient angles at each corner give a discreet Far Eastern déjà vu aspect to the whole. However, these exceptions to the rule actually provide a dose of variety, enriching the architectural scene, albeit incidentally, as happened when post-modernism officially hit architecture in 1980, when specific elements from historical traditions in modern architecture began to be used and accepted.

This aside, the world is suffering at the hands of mankind, now more than ever. Architecture and cities should make their own small contribution in order to urgently address this extremely serious issue. Bearing this in mind, it is surprising that the same building may be found in any part of the world, when climatic differences are specific criteria for differences in constructed images from one part of the world to another. Likewise, if eco-efficiency is considered necessary, it determines the distinctive use and availability of specific materials and methods in a particular place in order to achieve maximum energy savings.

Based on these considerations, we come across paradoxical situations: slate roofs are obligatory in certain villages in the Pyrenées because they are in line with popular traditional images, but the slate used is imported from Brazil, where it is cheaper than the slate from abandoned quarries in the area; a bank, in its bid for an image of modernity, builds a glass skyscraper in a city with a desert climate, but the building's surface gets so hot that the occupants cannot touch it without burning themselves.

It is therefore interesting to observe the latest additions to the global architectural scene from a modern-day, early 21st-century perspective. That is precisely the purpose of this book, which, through its analyses, leads to certain conclusions that we shall now examine.

To begin with, we can see in today's architecture, as in art, a reflection of the trends of the last few decades of the 20th century, albeit updated: a stroll around the latest art exhibits will reveal works of neo-expressionism, neo-abstractionism, neo-realism, neo-minimalism, neo-Dadaism, neo-surrealism, neo-conceptualism, neo-actionism and a host of other "neo-isms," as well as an intermingling of the early ideas of the various movements. In the same way, a stroll around the newest cities will reveal buildings based on 20th-century architectural trends, including certain features parallel to the concepts that contemporary art has been hatching for our now-globalized civilization.

In fact, the selection of works for this book is more than enough to provide this overall view—even more so considering that many of them are prize-winning works and among the most celebrated structures of recent years. For example, of the architects published here we can pick out two Pritzker Prize winners (tacitly considered architecture's Nobel Prize): Gehry and Koolhaas. Many others, also found in these pages, are equally deserving of this award, and are bound to receive it in future years; they include Calatrava, Diller & Scofidio, EMBT, Neutelings, Nouvel, Perrault, Rogers, Starck, and others.

Furthermore, it should be remembered that the world of architecture is special because public works that come to fruition usually start out as bids in public tenders, from which they emerge as the winner out of hundreds of

proposals, and this to some extent is indicative of their quality. In this book, quite a few of the works originated as winning bids in public tenders.

The projects selected for these pages are grouped into five chapters, depending on whether they are Urban Planning & Transport, Cultural Facilities, Leisure Facilities, Public Buildings, Institutions & Offices, and Homes. A sixth, concluding chapter makes a brief forecast, as it were, of the Architecture for the Future. This layout reproduces the sectorization of cities in accordance with use, a system that was first suggested a hundred years ago as the best solution for the problems faced by modern cities, and that Le Corbusier subsequently immortalized, at the beginning of the 1920s, with his functional division of cities into dwelling-work-recreation-circulation.

Current architecture defines not so much a diaphanous panorama of specific tendencies, as a quantity of architectural ideas that are added on a daily basis to a set of features that endow architecture with a unique, global quality, applicable to any context, in every corner of the five continents. In this respect, we can see in practically every contemporary work how functionalist principles are taken on, together with the use of modern materials—such as reinforced concrete, steel, and glass—in column structures, as defined by architects of the modernist movement in the early decades of the 20th century. Similarly, we have seen since then the ascendancy of elements such as the curtain wall or facades with glass panes from top to bottom, which have their origins in the factories that Walter Gropius designed in 1910 and 1914, and were subsequently refined in Ludwig Mies van der Rohe's glass skyscraper projects in 1919 and 1922. And so, you will find in these pages a good many current buildings with curtain walls, such as Skidmore, Owings & Merrill's Time Warner Center (New York) and Paul de Ruiter's Rijkswaterstaat Zeeland Head Office, the Head Office for the Department of Water Management & Traffic (Middelburg, Holland).

This practice, which originated from a reductionist viewpoint with the "less is more" that Ludwig Mies van der Rohe applied to his pure-glass structures, has aimed to consolidate itself since 1995 under the concept of the "light construction" that is typical of contemporary architecture, by adding to glass facades a spate of light-metal cladding.

It is because of Antonio Sant'Elia's manifesto of futurist architecture in 1914 ("oblique and elliptical lines are dynamic, and by their very nature possess an emotive power a thousand times stronger") or Erich Mendelsohn's statement ("function and dynamics, that's the challenge"), that one can find "rapid" lines, curves, that provide buildings with the perception of movement, the expression of speed, as may be seen in Carlos Zapata's family home (Miravalle, Ecuador), the UNStudio's Mercedes-Benz museum (Stuttgart, Germany), and Future Systems' Selfridges Birmingham building (Birmingham, U.K.).

Obviously, these projects could be attributed to one architectural tendency or another depending on their dominant features. Likewise, the architecture presented in this book has features that enable us to interpret certain works from an expressionist standpoint, such as Frank Gehry's MIT Stata Center (Cambridge, U.S.A.) and Aspect Studios's National Emergency Services Memorial (Canberra, Australia). Viewed from this perspective, they are all related to an awareness that has been growing since 1905, and that is expressed by statements such as Ernst Ludwig Kirchner's "My painting is a seismograph of my emotions."

At the same time, the predominant features of some works are more reductionist, hermetic, abstract, in other words, minimalist, as they were fondly described in critically acclaimed architecture since the late 1980s: works such as Marcio Kogan's Du Plessis Houses (São Paulo, Brazil) and Marco Savorelli's Grey Lounge (Brescia, Italy).

There are others who incorporate more humane concerns, which give a leading role to materials that are warmer, such as timber, and shapes that are softer. These acknowledge the concept of the humanization of architecture, which gained ground in the interwar period. Alvar Aalto in particular sought to make this concept compatible with modernity. It is represented by buildings such as Shim-Sutcliffe Architects' Muskoka Boathouse (Lake Muskoka, Canada), Miró Rivera's Guest House (Austin, Texas, U.S.A.) and Jonathan Levi Architects' May Residence (Brookline, Massachussetts, U.S.A.).

In addition, there is always room for buildings that are more figurative, even symbolic, such as Santiago Calatrava's Tenerife Auditorium (Santa Cruz de Tenerife, Spain), which freezes a moment between the static and the dynamic in its portrayal of a vast mythical bird on the point of taking flight—a concept this architect has touched on in a great many of his projects. And then there is Jean Nouvel and B720 Arquitectes' Agbar Tower (Barcelona, Spain), which

aims to emulate a waterspout (for the Barcelona Water Board) rising from the depths to above the Barcelona skyline. Or even EMBT Arquitectes Associats' Diagonal Mar Park (Barcelona, Spain), which is full of secret little metaphors.

There have been many examples of more technologically oriented architecture, in which technology becomes expression, throughout the 20th century, mainly due to the fascination that the machine has aroused in certain architects ever since the futurists introduced new ideals of beauty, something well illustrated by Filippo Tommaso Marinetti's claim: "a roaring car that seems to ride on grapeshot is more beautiful than the Victory of Samothrace." This tendency, which enjoyed considerable success from the 1980s onwards under the label of high tech is represented here in Richard Rogers and the Estudio Lamela's Madrid-Barajas Airport Terminal (Barajas, Spain).

In parallel, there has been a trend for a series of unusual, singular works in which what one might call typological and structural invention has been the most important factor. It is based on a search for a functional and constructive typology that renews the image of the function that a particular building has, as may be seen in the Neutelings Riedijk Architecten's Sphinxes Complex (Huizen, Holland).

This is the architectural mosaic of our planet. The same buildings are erected in any capital of the world, regardless of how much of a specific setting's historical or cultural baggage they may be carrying. Our history and culture are now global, common, linked by necessity, and following the same path. At the same time, they are inseparable, as Adolf Loos stated when he said: "today is built on yesterday, just as yesterday was built on the day before. It has never been any other way, and never will be."

It goes without saying that there are no significant examples of what has really been happening in the architectural vanguard and that the surface has just been scratched over the last five years. A trend that might be called digital organicism is converting latest-generation software into the new architectural resource. This has become the basis of a revolutionary system of projects and architectural production as well as a design tool; from this alliance, new organic forms have risen. "Digital tools and organic forms" is the international motto of this movement, a new architectural environment that has sprung up simultaneously in different parts of the world and spread all over the globe. It is also characterized by cyberecofusion, by its followers' particular attitude towards nature, and by the application of genetics and its processes. All this has led to it being labeled genetic architecture.

Alberto T. Estévez

Urban Planning
& Transport

Photo © Manuel Renau

Madrid-Barajas Airport

Barajas, Spain   2006

ARCHITECT
Estudio Lamela Arquitectos, Richard Rogers Partnership

CLIENT
AENA

PARTNERS
AENA (constructors); TPS, INITEC (engineering); Anthony Hunt Associates (structure design); OTEP Internacional (structural engineering); Arup (facade design)

CONSTRUCTED SURFACE AREA
General: 12,900,00 sq. ft. approximately
Terminal: 5,400,000 sq. ft. approximately
Satellite: 3,230,000 sq. ft. approximately
Parking: 3,340,000 sq. ft. approximately

COST
1,238 million euros

PROGRAM
New Air Transport Terminal Madrid-Barajas Airport

The new terminal of the Madrid-Barajas international airport is considered to be the largest construction project in Europe today. The idea was for it to be the new doorway to southern Europe, and it was to accommodate between 60 and 70 million travelers a year. This project for the airport was presented by four companies: the British based Richard Rogers Partnership, the Spanish studio of architecture, Estudio Lamela, the Spanish engineering firm Initec, and TPS from Britain, for an international competition held by AENA in 1997. The architectural design joins concepts like functionality, aesthetics, possibilities of future changes or extensions, user comfort, and an interaction with the environment of Madrid. The greatest of the architect's achievements resides in the materials used and in the suitable usage of the light, based on bamboo parasols and large glass skylights, and on an exterior roof composed of a double layer of aluminum, similar to a bird's extended wings, which harmonizes with the surroundings and reduces the impact on the environment.

The 12,900,000 sq. ft. surface area of the complex contains three buildings. The 3,340,000 sq. ft. parking lot has a 9,000-vehicle capacity. It is formed from six stories or independent metallic modules, joined visually using exterior cladding and lawn roofs, giving it the appearance of a garden when seen from above.

On entering the second building, the terminal, the undulating bamboo roof repeats the symbol of the figure of the bird outside. This floating fire-resistant bamboo structure creates warm and human indoor spaces and, with the help of the canyons and large cracks of light, which aid the natural lighting of the building's lower levels, the air quality is improved, and there is a natural environment with planted spaces. Everything is supported in the central area by a system of metal beams, which rest on a platform of reinforced concrete revealing the building's framework. The use of panoramic elevators and glass floors on the bridges allows the entry of light to be controlled, and provides better views of the exterior landscape, as is the case with the bamboo rods, which project different shadows as the sun changes position.

The terminal is for national flights and flights to countries within the European Union. Its

5,400,000 sq. ft. is spread over six levels, 74 check-in desks, and 38 aircraft contact points. There are three linear modules (check-in, processor, and docking station) fulfilling different functions depending on the flow of passengers (arrivals or departures).

The third building is the satellite, situated at the new runways and 2 km from the terminal, which deals with the rest of the international flights, with 3,230,000 sq. ft. surface area and 26 aircraft parking spaces. Despite the separation between the flow of international passengers and the flow of passengers from the Schengen zone, all users must pass through the Terminal building, since this is where the check-in and baggage collection is done. In this way, design and function are joined, which is reflected in the use of automated transport systems for travelers (elevators, escalators, and moving walkways), together with the automatic baggage handling system, which allows for the simultaneous movement of baggage and travelers. The satellite building is reserved for security control of international flights, their landings, and takeoffs.

This airport was designed as an environmental strategy in a space that has room to land 120 planes an hour, and considers the pollution and transit of passengers. This strategy is achieved using an opening in the structure to natural light, thereby reaching lower levels of energy consumption and a higher level of self-sufficiency. Maintenance costs are also lower due to the recycling of collected rainwater to water the green areas. Sustainability can be seen in the choice of material for the floor—limestone, which conveys warmth, is not very reflective and lessens the feeling of fatigue, making the terminal comfortable, operative, economical, and functional.

The canyons are the large openings made in the roof, that allow the entry of direct light. This changes depending on the time of day, and the effect is reinforced by glass floors on the bridges. In these open spaces, the vertical access points such as ramps, stairs and elevators, are connected to the horizontal ones: the metal bridges.

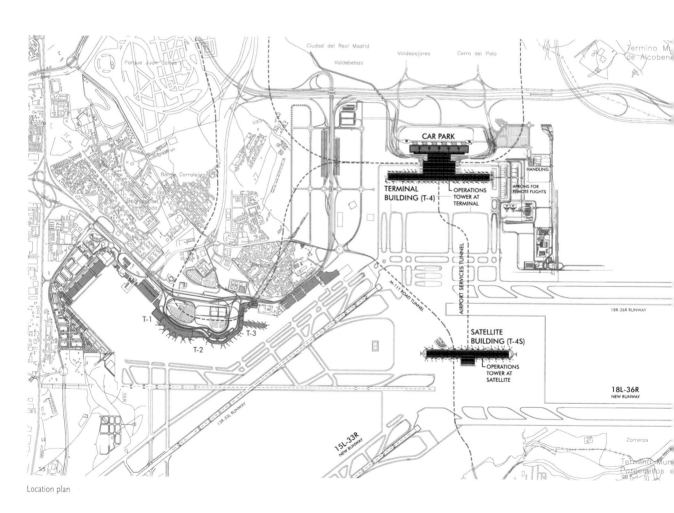

Location plan

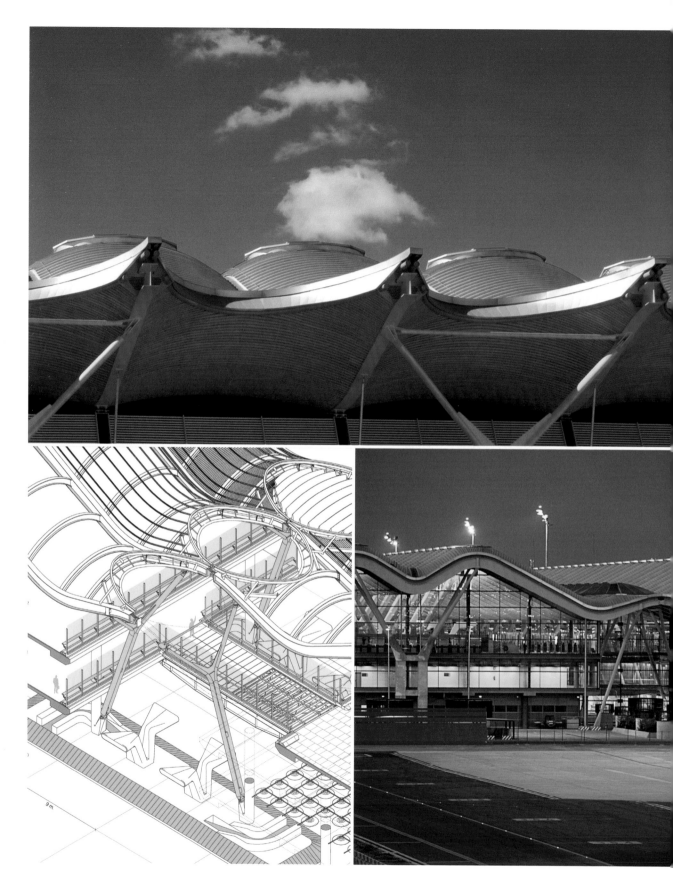

The singularity of the airport is its visible framework. Each module is composed of concrete beams, which allow for the creation of grids, all of which is covered in wide-edged metal beams. The Y-shaped pillars are the support points for the ends of the main beams.

Elevation

DEPARTURES

ARRIVALS

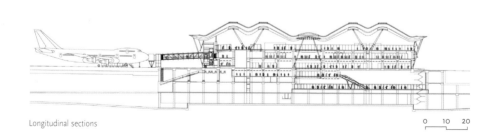

Longitudinal sections

0 10 20

Köln-Bonn Airport

Cologne, Germany   2000

ARCHITECT
Murphy/Jahn + Heinle, Wischer und Partner

CLIENT
Flughafen Köln/Bonn

PARTNERS
IGH Inenieurgemeinschaft Höpfner (enginee-ring); Ove Arup and Partners (steel); Werner obek Ingenieure (structure of the facade); Zimmermann + Schrage (mechanics); Institüt für Fassadentechnik IFFT (facade); Peter Andres (lighting); ICM Airport Technics (baggage); Prof. Karlsch (security)

CONSTRUCTED SURFACE AREA
General: 742,710 sq. ft.
Volume: 16,329,502 cu. ft.

PROGRAM
New Air Transport Terminal Köln-Bonn Airport

During the 90s, the number of passengers who landed using the only existing terminal at the Köln-Bonn Airport, had exceeded the 3 million annual capacity it was designed for. As a response to this problem the airport authorities decided to organize a design competition where solutions would be offered for the extension of the original terminal. Murphy/Jahn came up with a second terminal, which tackled the need to increase the airport's capacity to 7.5 million passengers per year. Two spaces were also included designated to parking areas, a two-level connection that joins the terminals, and an underground station for local and intercity trains.

There are many contrasts between the two terminals. While the first terminal was designed in the 60s, when there was less air traffic and security, and planes were smaller, the new terminal accommodates and organizes the flow of passengers arriving and leaving the airport better. This new structure is organized vertically in different levels: the underground train station occupies the two lowest levels, the arrivals corridor is located on level 3, boarding, duty-free shops and the connections with the parking on level four, and finally the departures corridor is located on the top level.

The new terminal 2 is an elongated volume that extends in a U shape from one of the existing arms in the old terminal. This enlarges the horizontal dimensions of the previous building. In contrast with the previous terminal, which was solid and concrete, the new building has been built from steel and prefabricated glass components, allowing the walls and roof to be transparent, lightweight and full of natural light. The concept is simple and easily visible to passengers leaving and arriving through the front doors and clear lines.

The routes that lead passengers to and from parking lot 2, along the raised walkway between terminals or from the train station to the terminal, are pleasant walks thanks to the lighting and ease the horizontal and vertical movement of passengers. When the construction was conceived it was decided to use prefabricated steel systems and components to increase the transparency and lightness of the building. The building consists of a 100-by-100 ft. structural module

that supports a continuously folded panel formed from panels or cells, which overlap on the roof, and includes skylights at the north end. These cells are designed to carry out various functions, such as to spread the weight, to protect against harsh weather conditions, to aid the exterior and interior absorption of heat and humidity, to deaden the acoustics, and to aid ventilation to avoid smoke buildup. The facade and the roof are no longer merely a constructive and decorative product; they are now a biological skin. Also, through these glass structures that allow natural light to enter throughout the terminal, there is a notable saving in energy. The facade is a structure of steel and light glass. The panels of insulating glass are supported at the joins by a spider-shaped structure. This technology of light glass is also applied to the bridges and handrails, the elevators, and to the floors and stairs.

The temperature controlling process is quite complex, taking advantage of outdoor temperatures for the interior, thereby maximizing the reduction in energy consumption. Parking lots 2 and 3 are clad in steel structures attached to a basic construction of robust steel. Stainless steel structures combine with others of perforated steel. The elevator towers are also steel structures with stainless steel platforms.

The train station is located at the heart of the airport and is lightly covered by an arched structure that supports a 660 ft. glass structure, which is projected towards the exterior. The station platform is 1360 ft. long and is situated 41.30 m below terminal 2 and the connections with terminal 1.

This renovation has converted the airport into a peripheral center, far from the city, with increasing importance in global networks, and into one of Germany's largest airports.

The use of glass both on the external facade and the roof allows natural light to enter, bathing the whole of the inside in light. This material is also used in passenger circulation areas, combined with another of the primary materials, stainless steel. These two materials allow for a lighter construction and a considerable reduction in energy consumption.

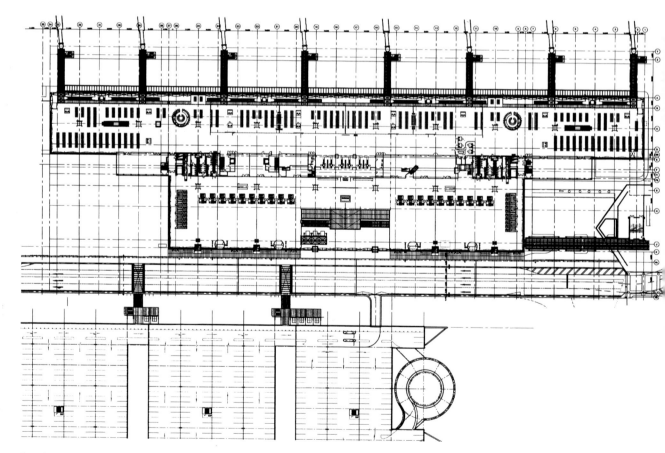

Floor plan

0   10

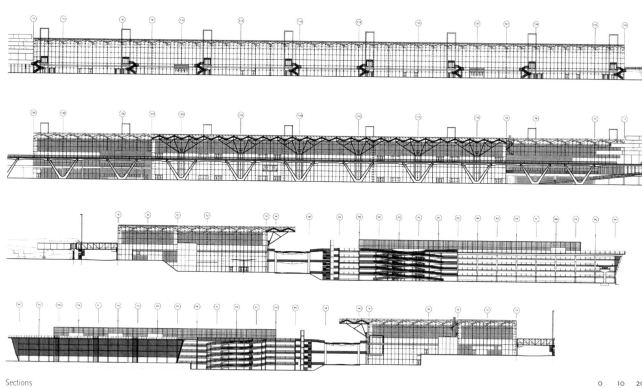

Sections

0 10 20

Photo © Despang Architekten

D-Line Train Stations

Hanover, Germany   2000

ARCHITECT
Despang Architekten

CLIENT
Transtec Bau Hannover

PARTNERS
ARUP, Dr. Burmester, Partners Garbsen (structural engineering), Fahlke & Dettmer (lighting engineering)

GENERAL FIELD
Thirteen train stations

VOLUME
Four to eight blocks making up each stop, measuring 9.8 ft. by 230 ft.

COST
8,600,000 euros

PROGRAM
Thirteen train stations affording access to public transport that ties the city to outlying districts. Also acting as the principal artery leading to the pavilions of the Hanover 2000 Universal Exhibition

The platforms for the D-South line of Hanover's city train system were built to cater to the large number of people visiting the Hanover 2000 Universal Exhibition, which took place between June 1 and October 31, focusing on three major concepts: nature, mankind, and technology. This major event has been held since the second half of the 19th century and was designed to show great technological and commercial inventions and the latest artistic trends, and to improve social communication between the world's peoples. Although more than one hundred and fifty years have passed since its inception, the spirit remains the same. The exhibitions focus on a specialized theme, run for three months at the most, and are endorsed and allocated by the Bureau International des Expositions (BIE). The Hanover Exhibition saw original international projects, new thematic pavilions, numerous activities, and national pavilions.

Cities hosting these universal exhibitions implement a city development plan to improve access for visitors and create new infrastructure and services.

This case called for the building of a new railway line to connect the city center with the exhibition location. A public tender was announced for construction of the platforms, and the winning bid came from Despang Architekten. This German architects' studio presented a project in which the stations had a serial design; each station was different, but the structure of the booths was the same: a standard frame made of steel with an opening to accommodate a seat. However, the materials used for the exteriors made each booth different. There were two main groups of material; the first included stone and brick, giving a closed finish, and the second included materials such as glass, timber and metal. The architects avoided using modular steel for the main structure because it would not dominate the unit as a whole and because it is a material that is quick to rust. For this reason, they chose more durable materials for the facings, given the nature of the surroundings and the vandalism rates for each area. Stainless steel is a commonly used material in the region's traditional houses, and copper, with its shades of green, blends in well with the landscape of the neighborhoods. The result is a simple design that precludes high maintenance costs for the railway.

For protection against the wind and rain, a small glass canopy was built standing on a row of steel columns. The simple but inventive structure of the stations dances along the route. Thus, the structures evoke typical features of the surroundings all along the line and establish associations in tune with the location. For example, each station is built using different materials to help tourists, passengers, users, and residents identify the stops. The D-South line is designed to let passengers see approaching trains at all times.

The choice of materials for the stations is governed by the architect's intention to integrate urban architecture into the surroundings. Lange-Feld Strasse station, whose structure is copper, treated with shades of green, blends naturally into the woody landscape all around. The architects also designed a shelter in the form of a portico to offer protection in bad weather.

FREUNDALLEE

KERSTINGSTRASSE

BULT

LANGE-FELD-STRASSE

PRESSEHAUS

BÜNTEWEG

THO UND SCHREBERGÄRTEN

NEUES WOHNGEBIET

EMSLANDSTRASSE

EDLES WOHNEN IN DEN OBSTGÄRTEN

SCHULE UND EXPOWOHNEN

IM ROHBERGE

SIEDLUNGSKEIM KRONSBERGQUARTIER

WÜLFERODER STRASSE

DATENVERARBEITUNGSGESELLSCHAFT

IN DER ENTHORST

VOR DEM EXPOTOR

STOCKHOLMER ALLEE

ZIEGELDIKTIERTES GEWEBE

HETEROGENES WOHNEN

KINDERKRANKENHAUS UND TENNISPLÄTZE

SCHREBERGÄRTEN UND BESSERE STADTTEILE

HALTESTELLE VERLAGSGESELLSCHAFT

/AM WÄLDCHEN

KERNSTADT

PERIPHERIE

EXPO WOHNQUARTIER

Location plan

Steel was used to build the frames of the stations, and different materials were chosen for the facings. The architects wanted to distinguish two types of facing according to the materials used: stone and brick; and timber, glass and metal.

Photo © H. G. Esch, Kohn Pedersen Fo

Mori Tower (Roppongi Hills)

Tokyo, Japan   2003

ARCHITECT
KPF – Kohn Pedersen Fox Associates

CLIENT
Mori Building Company

PARTNERS
*Erie Miyaki Architects and Engineers
(associated architects); Mori Building
Company (constructors)*

AREA
3,530,000 sq. ft.

COST
3,200 million euros (Roppongi Hills in total)

PROGRAM
*The Roppongi Hills housing development inclu-
des offices, an art museum, residential area,
hotel, theater, cinema, television studio, shops,
metro, parks, etc.*

The Mori Tower forms part of an enormous housing estate called Roppongi Hills, situated along the Roppongi Dori, one of the main thoroughfares of the Japanese capital. This urban development was built under one of the largest construction magnates, Minoru Mori. The complex is formed from a surface area of 3,015,000 sq. ft. of offices, the hotel Grand Hyatt Tokyo with 380 bedrooms, the residential estate Roppongi Hills, shops, restaurants, cinemas, a television studio, an amphitheater, the Corn Museum, a metro station, and various parks.

The 780-feet Mori Tower stands out in this important commercial and leisure district, with its 58 multipurpose stories, six of which are underground. On the top ten floors are the most important sections of a more public and tourist use. This is the case for floor 52, where the Tokyo city view offers panoramic views, both during the day and night, over the city from 820 meters above sea level. The Mori Arts Museum is installed on the 53rd floor, designed by Gluckman Mayner for contemporary art exhibitions of a wide variety of styles and artists, both Japanese and foreign. This museum is designed to accommodate

around 20,000 visitors per day. On floor 54, an open-air area has been built to act as a viewing platform, offering spectacular views over the city. The less commonly used and more private Roppongi Hills Club occupies the 51st floor, with eight restaurants, clubs, and bars that offer panoramic views over the city as well as entertainment. The Roppongi Academy Hills contains installations that see to the intellectual needs of the inhabitants and functions as a school, private bookshop for the members of the institution, cultural center, and conference area.

The tower is situated on a hill that borders traffic, making it appear higher than it really is. The lighting that surrounds the building imitates a graphic equalizer moving in time with the music. The aesthetics of the tower follow in the wake of other contemporary Japanese constructions and the Japanese tradition of representing natural forms with geometric patterns, like changing cubist volumes. The upper part of the building and the base draw on the folded paper of Japanese origami, while the framework of the building is reminiscent of a samurai's armor.

The materials most used in the building work, apart from concrete, are steel and a glass curtain wall that wraps around the entire building. In the constructions at the foot of the tower, warm, horizontal, limestone volumes have been chosen. This makes the tower's vertical volumes contrast horizontally with the buildings at the base, as is the case with the colors of the metal and limestone. This way the tower is more solid at its base and more transparent on the upper floors.

Roppongi Hills is known as The Arteligent City, where art and intelligence are fused. The Mori tower was chosen, in 2003, as one of the best new skyscrapers.

The volumes of the hotel and theater situated at the lower part and surrounding the Mori tower act as a single unit and enhance the chromatic metallic palette of the tower. Also, the vertical form of the tower contrasts with the expansive limestone horizontal structures. The tension generated by these opposing elements creates a highly pronounced, striking angle, which is visible from all the adjacent streets.

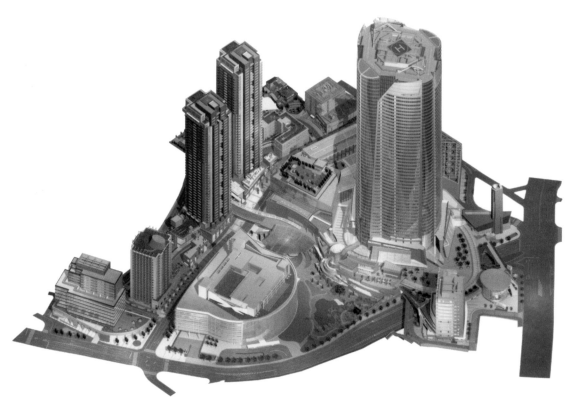

Axonometry

The singularity of the Mori Tower resides in being turned into an icon on Tokyo's skyline, thanks to its volumes, which change depending on the angle from which they are seen. For example the base and the upper part draw directly on traditional Japanese shapes, like samurai armor.

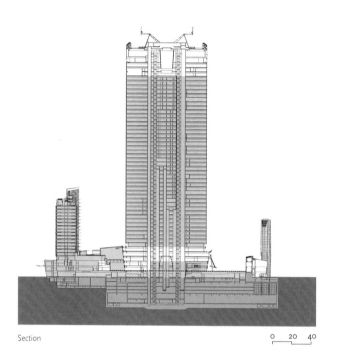

Section

0   20   40

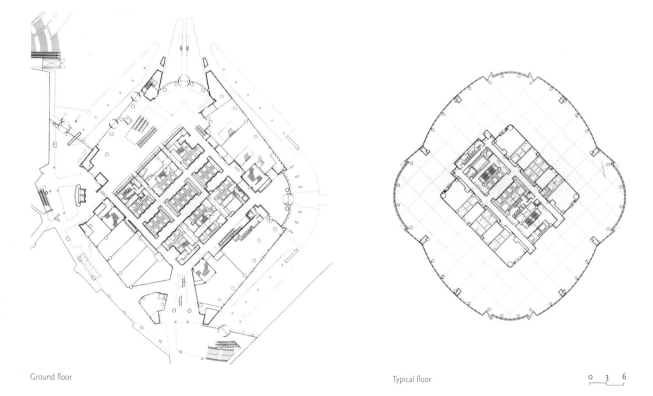

Ground floor

Typical floor

0   3   6

Photo © Andrew Hoobs, Adrian Lander, Peter Clarke, Trevor Mei

Federation Square

Melbourne, Australia   2004

ARCHITECT
LAB Architecture Studio, Bates Smart

CLIENT
Federation Square Management

PARTNERS
Multiplex (managing contractor); Karres en Brands (landscape architects); Atelier One (engineers); Atelier Ten, Connell Wagner, Hyder Consulting, Bonacci Group

CONSTRUCTED SURFACE AREA
General area: 3.6 ha.
Construction area: 473,600 sq. ft.

COST
283 million euros

PROGRAM
The architectural space Federation Square includes an amphitheatre, a square, an atrium, an art gallery, a cinema, various museums, and design centers

The urban architectural space Federation Square has been conceived as a new social, political, and cultural center and is located in the very center of the city. In just a few years, it has become a landmark for the people who live here and exceeded expectations, becoming one of the main tourist destinations in Australia, with 20 million visitors a year. This is mainly thanks to its strategic location in the heart of the city and to its creation as a commemorative object for the centenary of the Federation (2001). It is the true generator of all cultural and community activity in this Australian city.

LAB architecture studio won the international design competition that was organized in 1996. On a site intact for construction purposes, the architecture studio designed a place where elements and activities of different natures would come together, while maintaining formal and above all visual cohesion. In this sense the composite proposal of the architects is in accordance with the true spirit of the federation, known for bringing independent and individual entities together, which, when combined, form a single collective. In the same way the project contributes to cultural and public-minded togetherness, a place where the visitors interact with local passers-by and workers. Federation Square is composed of nine buildings dedicated to specific cultural and commercial functions, such as restaurants, cafes, bars, and art centers. In this place, more than 2,000 activities and events are organized throughout the year. The Square is the central point from which all the parties and festival events, which take place outside, emerge and develop and has a capacity of 35,000 people at any one event. All of the flooring is done with Australian sandstone cobbles. Due to the sloping terrain, a small pitched elevation was built to gain panoramic views of the city and river. At its highest point, a giant video screen has been installed that livens up the square for passers-by. One of the main buildings that integrate the main square is the BMG Edge, located by the atrium close to the river. This place, with a seating capacity of between 290 and 450 people, is an amphitheatre designed for theatrical performances, musical events, presentations, and brand launches.

After this is the Atrium, a glass, steel, and zinc structure in the form of a great arch,

back to back with the Ian Potter Centre: NGV Australia. The Ian Potter building is dedicated exclusively to showing work from Australian artists in more than 20 galleries. This area also accommodates cafeterias, bars, and shops, which have direct access either to the River Yarra or to the main square. This urban set up draws literally on the traditional and historical town planning of the city. On one side of the Square is the Australian Centre for the Moving Image, dedicated to the pre-cinema image up to the most modern digital media. Two multi-format cinemas and a specialized cinematographic gallery were built inside this building. Another building is dedicated to Australia's champions, called Champions: Australian Racing Museum and Hall of Fame, exhibiting the grandiose collection of objects related to Racing in Australia. The National Design Centre reflects all forms of expression of contemporary Australian design. As well as promoting activities, it acts as a documentation center, with galleries for exhibiting and selling artistic work. Capping the list of large buildings in Federation Square is the Melbourne Visitor Center as the tourist information center for the city of Melbourne and Victoria.

The formal conception the architects were aiming at was the material and visual coherence of all the buildings using perfectly assembled geometric structures arranged irregularly. The rectangle and triangle are the most frequently used geometric shapes in the different buildings, as glass, stone and zinc are the main materials used. Following the new models of global architecture, systems that would allow a considerable energy saving were sought, such as that of the atrium. Inside is a passive cooling system for the summer months, which lowers the temperature to be up to 12 degrees cooler than that of the exterior.

Victoria's National Gallery presents the most comprehensive collection of Australian art, from the aborigines to more recent works or art, within 78,300 sq. ft. of exhibition space. The south facade exemplifies this original grill structure laid out irregularly, allowing for a changing surface thanks to malleable materials like zinc, sandstone, and glass.

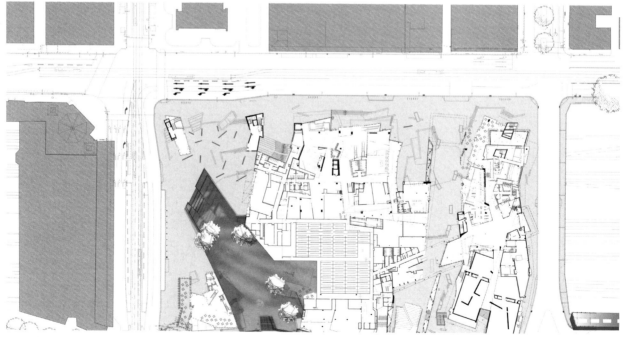

Location plan

*In Flinders Street, which runs around the square, the back facades of some
of the buildings in Federation Square can be seen. From left to right are:
the National Gallery of Victoria, the Atrium, and the Australian Center for
the Moving Image. This unique collection of surfaces and visible shapes in
the buildings offers a changing configuration and orientation.*

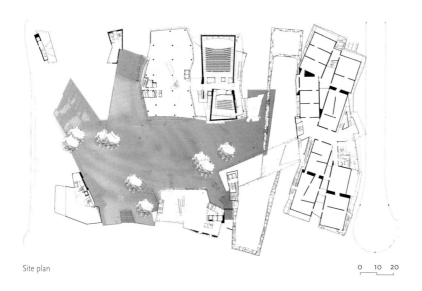

Site plan

0   10   20

0   5

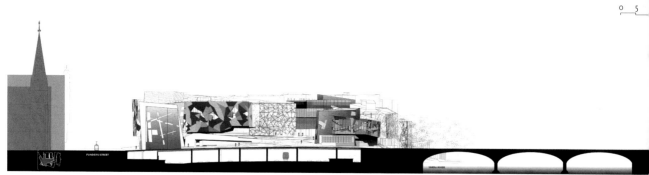

Elevations

0   5

Photo © Neil Fo

30 Adelaide Street East

Toronto, Ontario, Canada   2002

ARCHITECT
Janet Rosenberg & Associates, Quadrangle Architects

CLIENT
Dundee Reality Management Corp.

CONSTRUCTORS
Aldershot Landscape Contractors

SURFACE AREA
0.23 ha.

COST
469,000 euros

PROGRAM
Rest area and public garden

This work is situated in the center of Toronto and acts as a public garden, rest area, and intimate interior courtyard to a recently renovated office building. The construction follows the same palette of colors and above all, the use of the same materials as those used in the building. This allows the atrium to integrate perfectly with its surroundings, without interfering in the routine or daily activities of the workers or passers-by. The client expressed his intention to the architects that he wanted to develop a design indicative of the brand, reflected in an international-style office building. To achieve this objective, a space that would be pleasant for the user was created, which would be easily recognized from the city's urban panorama and visible from the street. In short, a landmark in the city. To enhance this unique, aesthetic identity a range of furniture and plant pots were incorporated into the main atrium, which add a touch of nature to this urban space.

The landscape architecture, within an urban setting, is composed of a central courtyard or atrium, an outdoor meeting area, and various secondary spaces created using the

relation between the building and its position. Two original, enormous and majestic ginkgo trees preside over the central courtyard, which were there originally and were preserved throughout the construction. Between the two trees is a central, covered granite passageway in the shape of an arch, delineated on both sides by two stainless steel walls. This path leads the visitor towards the main entrance to the office block. On one side is a type of small lake with straight and rectangular forms and a series of perfect limestone cubes installed and distributed around it. These cubes, separated from each other, are arranged at the edge so people can sit and observe their urban environment. The water springs from one of the stainless steel walls that delineate the tree and central passageway. The function of the water here is to bring something natural to the environment, as well as the relaxing sensation produced by the sound of the water falling in the small pool. Furthermore, to harmonize even more with the surroundings, original designs, created especially for the occasion, have been created for the large plant pots which containing small

plants and bushes. These pots add color to the existing chromatic combination of grays and silvers of the stainless steel and granite. With the passing of time and since its finish, the place has been intensely used by the employees and visitors of the city, and has achieved its objective, which was to become a recognizable space within Toronto's urban environment. This urban landscape has been categorized as revolutionary, having been carried out at the highest level with the introduction of new, previously unused materials like stainless steel, which is undoubtedly the star of the space. This material dominates the work and gives the space identity, challenging the perception of the public interested in landscape design and even that of landscape architects. Also, the architects have maximized the level of the urban furniture, treating it as if it were a sculptural work. They are sculptural pieces designed and used as decorative elements, while also integrating with the landscape.

This way, the architectural space is a separate element from the main building, conceptually speaking. It is a true example of how to integrate and join art and landscaping to create a space, which is both functional and pleasant, yet with its own unique identity, and all this right in the heart of a large city.

In a high-speed and stressful working environment a space has been built between office blocks that is relaxing and full of harmony. Following the same formal line used in the main building, stainless steel is used as the main construction material in this landscape. Also cubes of limestone were created to act as seats, allowing visitors to take a breath during their hectic daily lives.

Photo © Gustafson Guthrie Nichol

The Lurie Garden

Chicago, IL, U.S.A.   2004

ARCHITECT
Gustafson Guthrie Nichol

CLIENT
Millenium Park

PARTNERS
Walsh Construction (constructors); McDonough Associates, KPFF Consulting (engineering); Robert Israel, Piet Oudolf, Spectrum Strategies, CMS Collaborative, Schuler & Shook, Ferry Guen Design Associates

CONSTRUCTED SURFACE AREA
135,940 sq. ft.

PROGRAM
Botanical and decorative garden belonging to the Lakefront Millenium Park

This recreational area called The Lurie "Shoulder" Garden is an ambitious landscaped construction that forms part of the Lakefront Millenium Park, in a historical area known as Chicago's Gran Park. It is situated among various emblematic constructions, more precisely connecting the partly covered bandshell from Frank O. Gehry & Associates and the Chicago Art Institute designed by Renzo Piano Building Workshop.

The garden pays homage to a well-known slogan in this city "Urs in Horto" (City in a Garden); referring to the transformation this city went through from its marshy origins to a well-known, powerful and important metropolis.

One of the garden's most noteworthy and marvelous features is the theatrical lighting of the 4-meter-high Shoulder Hedge. The garden is formed from diverse sections, which are very different from one another. One of the most striking is the Extrusion Plaza, the extension that acts as an axis to north-south circulation through the Millenium Park. It links with Monroe Street, and to the southeast with the Exelon Pavilion, continuing to the north towards Pritzker Pavilion

and the rest of the Millenium Park. As the main route of circulation, the design of the Extrusion Plaza makes reference to the movement of the city's and the region's prime industry, the automobile and transport industry, in short the city's industrial character. The Shoulder Hedge is the most characteristic of the landscaping. This 14 ft. botanical and decorative garden boasts a gigantic, thick hedge that circulates the interior of the garden from the north to the south. This structure, called Big Shoulders Hedge, is a living wall that protects the perennial nature from the intense and incessant traffic of people that move around Millenium Park, and surrounds the garden on both sides. It is defined using a metal structure or armature that gives shape to the various types of vegetation, and is regularly pruned to maintain a precise curved outline. The vegetation is always at the same height and never escapes its armature; this protects the hedges from the crowds of people. The only growth that is allowed is upwards so the visitors can observe the development of the plants.

Another important part of the garden is the West Hedge, where there are decorative and

original forms, that didactically explain the Greek myth of the nymph Dafne, who escaped Apollo and when trapped transformed into laurel. In contrast with the mythological references, the futuristic appearance of the Garden is seen with the natural surroundings to promote urban growth, industry, and agriculture. Thus there is a definite contrast between the Mythological story of Apollo (symbol of industrial power) and Dafne (symbol of beauty), with today's Chicago (symbol of urban power) and the garden (symbol of the natural environment). The Dark Plate is the most nostalgic, mysterious and cool place. Here the beginnings of the place are told, and further-

more those of the city. This site started off as the delta of a river with a wild coastline. Another relevant spot inside this Lurie Garden is the Seam, which acts as a promenade. It is not a public thoroughfare, but a place to take an occasional walk. The Seam occupies the area where the containing walls previously stood, creating a border between the lake and the land. There is also a 5 ft. wide strip of water running along the vertical wall of the Dark Plate. The Boardwalk, constructed from resistant ipe wood, forms a 2 ft. wide step, which becomes a spontaneous seat for visitors to feel the water in a much more intimate and refreshing way.

The lighting is one of the most important and striking features of this garden. At night the Lurie Garden becomes a subtle, luminous container of light, where the paths are brightly lit by lights built into the ground. This lighting creates a magical, theatrical atmosphere, focused on those spaces that invite visitors to enter the space.

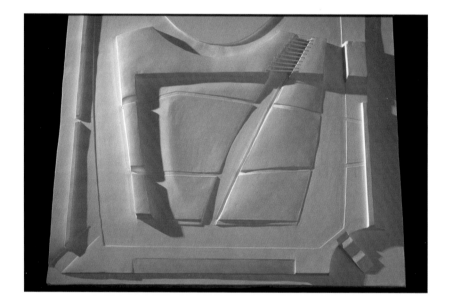

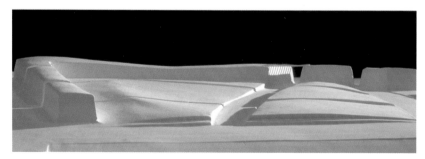

Models

Photo © Roger Casa

Diagonal Mar Park

Barcelona, Spain   2002

ARCHITECT
EMBT – Enric Miralles Benedetta Tagliabue Arquitectes Associats

CLIENT
Diagonal Mar Hines

PARTNERS
Elena Rocchi, Lluis Cantallops, Fabián Asunción (project managers); Edad Londres (landscape architects); Òscar Tusquets, Xavier Sust (urban architects); Benjumea (constructors); Europroject Consultores Asociados, José María Velasco (engineering)

AREA
14 ha.

PROGRAM
Large park for taking walks, relaxing and for children to play in

The Diagonal Mar Park is situated between Diagonal Avenue and Nova Mar Bella beach in Barcelona. It is in response to the need for an outdoor recreational, relaxing area for the families that live in this new part of Barcelona. The area is the result of the renovation of an industrial zone. More precisely, the park occupies the site of an old metal works factory where they used to build trains, trams, carriages for the metro, and escalators. It is a nearby, accessible park, like the garden or recreational courtyard of any of the houses in the neighborhood. The architects designed the park as a large network of paths that start at a central point and run in all directions of the space, like the branches of a tree. Man's life path was also a source of inspiration. When the architects visited the place it rained, giving them the thought of using water as the main element throughout. To honor the name, Diagonal Mar, they wanted the water to reach the Diagonal.

Starting at the sea and heading towards the Diagonal are two main axes that act as routes around the park. The first is the main path through the Park like a Rambla (boulevard), typical of the city, and which is used

by a large number of people. This main path connects Diagonal and the beach, crossing the Ronda Litoral (the periphery road) via a pedestrian bridge situated at the start of the park. This main path also follows the edge of a large lake, which together with the area of trees, are the most characteristic, identifying elements of the park and those that give it its character. On this large surface of water are various fountains and waterfalls, etc. By installing vegetation at the edges, the water is oxygenated, thereby allowing the incorporation of animal life. Also, the placement of this lake, close to the path, transforms it into a place for recreation where lovers of toy boats can freely practice their favorite game. The dominant salt marsh-style vegetation in the lake develops as if it were at sea. The reeds grow in height and density eventually reaching the adjacent streets.

The second main axis is based on the other source of inspiration for the architects: the stages of a man's life. Man is born from water as the park leaves the beach by the sea. Man's infancy is then reflected in the children's recreational play area. Music and fitness equipment occupy this small area. Man,

after childhood, reaches adolescence, which in the park takes the form of the area called The Magic Mountain. On this mountain there are various slides installed where children of all ages can join in the fun. To finish, man becomes an adult, socializing and forming relations with other adults, which is reflected in the citizen participation area. For the design of this adult zone, the architects wanted to involve the neighbors by carrying out a process of citizen participation in which more than a thousand people would collaborate. From the many proposals, they finally settled on the amphitheatre and sport areas. Throughout the park are small squares where a series of large clay vases with flow-

erpot holders join with the vegetation as if it were someone's back garden. These large vases covered with *trencadís* (Catalan mosaics) are lithographed with a pop aesthetic and bring color to the whole space.

The Diagonal Mar Park is the first park to apply criteria of sustainable development. In fact it is Barcelona's first ecological park. This environmental angle can be seen in the use of ground water for watering and the ponds, the use of local species that consume less water and are easily maintained, the intelligent control of the water in the fountains and the lighting, and, finally, the use of sand from the excavations carried out during the construction.

This park is not the typical city park but boasts extensive stretches of lawn and innovatively designed benches and sculptures. Some 1,005 native trees grow in the park, which consume little water and are easily maintained. This 150-year-old drago canario stands out at the end of the only bridge across the lake.

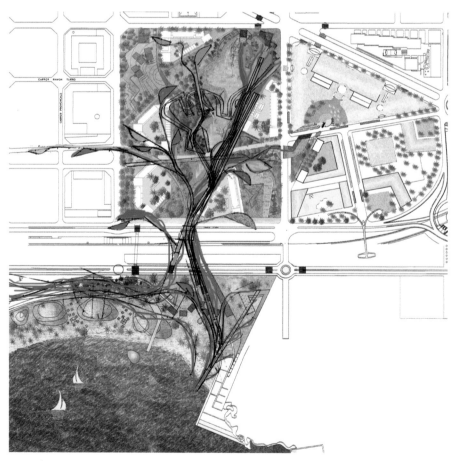

Location plan

The most frequently used materials in the Diagonal Mar Park are steel in the large pergolas formed from cables and pipes, and clay in the large flowerbeds decorated with pop-style tiles. Water is the main feature of the space, and is reflected in both the large lake and the smaller ones, creating a space of 130,440 sq. ft.

Photo © Jean Michel Landec

Cardada Intervention

Locarno, Switzerland   2001

ARCHITECT
Paolo L. Bürgi

CLIENT
Cardada Impianti Turistici, Orselina-Locarno

PARTNERS
*Passera & Pedretti Engineers (promontory);
Stoffel Engineering (observatory); Mario
Codoni, Markus Felber, Paolo Oppizzi
(geology); Guido Maspoli, Bellinzona (biology);
Bertea (history)*

COST
18 million euros

PROGRAM
*Various construction projects in the Cardada
mountains of the Swiss Alps*

Cardada is mainly a summer mountain resort that offers visitors a wide variety of activities, like excursions, treks, relaxation areas, and playgrounds, within a setting of great natural beauty.

This project consists of different, isolated structures along a path that leads to the summit of Cardada, at 4,400 ft. above sea level. This guided walk leads visitors slowly through beautiful landscapes and delicate nature before arriving at an impressive lookout from where they can soak up the Swiss mountain scenery. At the beginning of the path, the architect built a main square, a hard design composed of an area covered in granite. It is an attempt to interpret the traditional material of the adjacent valleys in a new and very precise way. A lawn has been laid between the rows of granite tiles. On the same square is a fountain made from a tree trunk, which contrasts with the strict simplicity and hardness of the floor. A long and wide wooden bench borders the square where visitors can rest and reflect. Its basic form adapts and connects with the geometry of the floor and, also, indicates the angles where the paths wind their way

toward the summit. The square is the place where the people meet, chat, and talk about excursions, and it is also a refuge for those starting off on the trip. This design reflects the architect's reference to leaving the city behind and being in the countryside.

Following this, new connecting paths were built, with the idea of being the backbone along which visitors can experience the surroundings dominated by the lush nature filled with trees. There are silver fir trees, darkly colored, humid and cold, and beeches with gray trunks and dry foliage—in short, large trees, joyful and full of life, and saturated with sunlight. This route of half a mile circulates the hill from east to west and alerts the visitor's senses to colors, smells, tastes, sounds, and textures in an entirely natural environment. To deepen this awakening of the senses, a series of games have been installed along the path, designed both for adults and children.

This path leads walkers to a small square where they find a suspended walkway. It is a construction made from steel and titanium that rises between the trees and leads to an observation platform. From this lookout, apart from contemplating the surrounding

mountains, visitors can enjoy views over Lake Maggiore. Along the way to the platform, visitors find small symbols on the tiles that cover the walkway reminding them how fragile the surroundings are. This idea is reinforced using brief explanatory texts in the fenced off area with information about these mysterious symbols. Here is where all the intentions, ideas and principles, foundations for the formation and creation of the space, come together: the perception of landscape, history, literature, and ecology.

The last piece of work is in the Geological Observatory, accessed via chairlift at the 5,480-foot Cimetta peak. Strips of rock were raised that stretch down the sides to a round platform, 50 ft. in diameter. A red line penetrates the middle of the platform dividing it in two and simulating a chronological line, where stones of different materials lie. It is an explanation of how millions of years ago some stones got separated from others. The purpose of this observatory is to give the visitor easier access to the history, allowing him to think freely. The experience helps us understand how short the human life is compared with the immense scale of life on our planet through the ages and eras.

The visitor's first stop on arriving at Cardada is the Main Square covered with slate paving alternated with straight stretches of grass. Another of the projects in this area is the steel and titanium walkway, which seems to float and appear through the trees, becoming a lookout point towards Switzerland's Lake Maggiore.

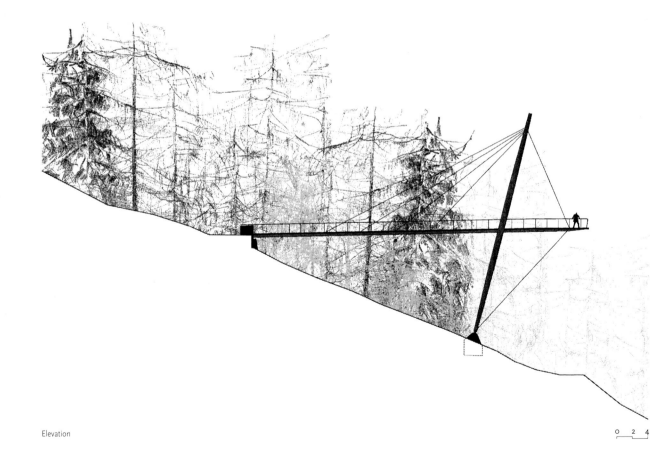

Elevation

0 2 4

Photo © Barnett Photograph

Central Indianapolis Waterfront

Indianapolis, IN, U.S.A.   2006

ARCHITECT
Sasaki Associates

CLIENT
City of Indianapolis, State of Indiana, US Army
Corps of Engineers (Louisville District)

PARTNERS
Beaty Construction, Milestone Construction
(construction)

OVERALL SURFACE AREA
9 miles (river course)

COST
92 million euros

PROGRAM
Urban development for a period of 13 years-plus
along the bank of the White River as it passes
through Indianapolis

The landscape project assigned to the architects was the development of the bank of the White River as it passes through the city of Indianapolis. This intervention transformed the city river boundary into a unified system of open spaces, which in turn was used to link the city's main civic centers with the riverbank. Since it was opened, this process of unification has enabled the waterfront to become a landmark for the inhabitants of the city as well as a landscape that will keep its place in the city's tangible and collective memory.

The site was transformed into an area of great scenic beauty in keeping with the recreational activities carried out in the area, and has answered the needs of the inhabitants who were asking for an area to be set aside for public use.

For the urban area covering more than 9 miles on the banks of the White River, the architects came up with a general plan that would affect the entire waterfront. The project entailed minimizing the sensation of the river being separated from the city through the creation of enormous dykes, floodwalls, and huge locks. To do this, long walkways

were constructed for the public on both sides of the river and all along the river course. These walkways are designed to facilitate physical access to this area from the downtown area of the city.

The main organizational element of the place is the extension of the historical Central Canal, which was previously renovated in the 1980s. This extension emerges in a dock, which greatly reduces the volume of water, to eventually become a kind of small gutter. This gutter redirects the water until it flows into a spring that empties out directly into the river. The most important open space designed for public use on the whole site is the main park, known as the Capital City Landing. The park is built on various levels beside snatches of pathway, bridges, industrial warehouses, and business premises, useful corridors, canals and floodwalls, with logical and obviously superimposed buildings marking the existence of 175 years of industrial activity. Taking the history of the site and the previous architectural conditions as their starting point, the designers reinterpreted the forms of all these elements, giving the area a very contemporary look.

Another of the open spaces that forms a key element in this project is the National Road Promenade. This river promenade follows on from Indianapolis Road and becomes the main pedestrian route going from the riverbank right into the downtown area of the city. The path ends at the terrace known as McCormick, where homage is paid to the first bridge to be built across the river and also to the place where a famous colonial cabin was erected. South of this river walk is the nerve center of the whole urban development: Celebration Plaza. This plaza is orientated towards the river by means of a grass and stone amphitheater that breaks up the visual monotony of the floodwall between the spring and the eastern side, near the old bridge on Washington Street. This restored bridge connects with the plaza by means of a new gateway to Indianapolis Zoo. Apart from the development of the surrounding

area, the design, construction, and conception of this new public area makes it easier for specific areas along the riverbank to be developed and to grow in importance. This is the case of the new IMAX Theater, the State Museum, a baseball stadium, and several buildings adjacent to the zoo.

At the Central Indianapolis Riverfront three important crucial objectives have been achieved. The first of these is that the site functions as a magnet for revitalizing the downtown area of the city. The second is the growing enthusiasm for private and public investments. The third objective consists of attracting private capital to trigger the development of residential districts downtown. However, the most important aspect of the project is that it has fulfilled the main mission for which it was designed: the river area has become the true heart of the city of Indianapolis.

All along the route leading from the downtown area of the city to the bank of the White River, a series of public open spaces have been built at key sites connecting the walkways along the riverbanks with the adjacent urban structure. These places have acquired a leading role in the city on their own account, although their integration with the surrounding area is clear, both visually and materially.

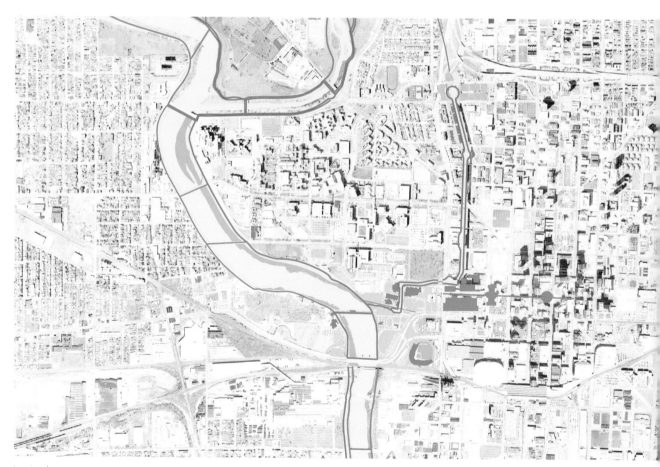

Location plan

Photo © Aljosa Brajdic, 3LHD Archi•

Memorial Pedestrian Bridge

Rijeka, Croatia   2001

ARCHITECT
Studio 3LHD

CLIENT
Rijeka City Council (Croatia)

PARTNERS
*GP Krk (general building constructors);
Shipyard 3.Maj (steel construction work); Almes
(aluminum, glass); Ribaric (lighting); CES doo
Rijeka-Jean Wolf, Zoran Novacki (engineering)*

SIZES
*Overall: 154.2 ft
Length: 117.1 ft
Width: 17.7 ft
Thickness: 2.1 ft
Height: 29.5 ft*

COST
948,000 euros

PROGRAM
*Monumental bridge to commemorate the
Croatian soldiers who took part in the Balkan
War*

This monumental bridge is located in the city of Rijeka, on the northern coast of Croatia. This is an important port linking Central Europe with the countries bathed by the Adriatic Sea. The erection of this monument stems from the desire to pay tribute to the Croatian soldiers who took part in the Balkan War in the 1990s. It was from Rijeka that many volunteer soldiers set out to reach the borders of Croatia. The city also offered shelter to the refugees from the interior of the country who came looking for safety in the cities along the Adriatic coast. A specific spot has been set aside at the monument for the public to place their flowers, candles, and other tributes.

What makes the bridge really outstanding is the fact that it has been conceived as an architectural element that has a clearly monumental design. Its purely functional appearance as a transit zone linking the two banks of the canal, which is typical of this type of urban infrastructure, was also given the category of commemorative monument. It achieves the idea of being a monument by the verticality of the bridge at one end. It runs from the historical old city, over the

canal and finishes on the opposite bank, in the area of the old port. This port is currently used for parking, but it will be converted into a municipal park in the not-too-distant future. This area has taken on so much importance that it has become an architectural landmark for the inhabitants of the city and is also used as a social meeting point.

The Memorial Bridge was designed as a very thin horizontal structure crossing the canal in a characteristic L-shape. Most of the elements were industrially manufactured and assembled on site. There was a barge available that was specially designed to remain semisubmerged in the water to take the weight of the bridge. Furthermore, the barge enabled the structure to be transferred across the various bridges already in existence. Most of the parts were manufactured at a local steelworks, where 150 tons of material was produced for the bridge. Once all the elements had been assembled, the structure was removed, enabling the work to be carried out while the tide was low. At each end of the river banks vertical compression pylons were erected, these being the elements that really take the weight of the main beam. The mate-

rial used mainly consists of steel, which makes up a large part of the bridge, with an overall length of 154.2 ft. A steel and magnesium alloy is also used, as is a huge glass balustrade with a wooden handrail that runs the length of the walkway and acts as a support and safety element for the pedestrians. These materials, which endow the monument with a chromatic effect that is very unusual in this type of intervention, were necessary to guard against corrosion, which is caused by the salt from the seawater.

The monument appears to be of simplistic design, but it has enormous visual impact, both during the day and also at night time. In daylight hours it takes on the appearance of a smooth slab of stone, polished and pure, standing out above its surroundings as if it were detached from the earth. This same sensation is heightened at night, when there is a peaceful atmosphere, an effect that is achieved thanks to the cold LED lights reflecting in the water.

This hybrid between urban design and public usage completely changed the district's image in both a physical and symbolic fashion. It has become an architectural landmark in the city and also serves to identify and represent it, distinguishing it from other towns along the coast.

Besides its functional purpose as a pedestrian walkway linking the two banks of the Croatian city of Rijeka, the Memorial Pedestrian Bridge has been designed by its architects as a monument commemorating the Croatian soldiers who fought to defend their country. The result is an architectural element with an enormous visual impact that has changed the face of the city.

Construction system diagrams

Photo © Ben Wrigl

National Emergency Services Memorial

Canberra, Australia   2004

ARCHITECT
Aspect Studios

CLIENT
National Emergency Service Personnel Sterring Committee & National Capital Authority

PARTNERS
Charles Anderson (artist); Darryl Cowie (development and construction); Martin Butcher (lighting design); SA Precast (construction of the wall); John Woodside Consulting (engineering)

SURFACE AREA
5.382 sq. ft.

COST
798,000 euros

PROGRAM
Monument erected in tribute to the Australian Emergency Services

The commemorative monument was erected in the Australian capital, right in the magnificent boulevard known as Anzac Parade. It is in this avenue that the most important public buildings and monuments of the city have taken up their position over the years. With the building of the Emergency Services Memorial the place is bestowed with a new aesthetic and psychological significance for the city's inhabitants. The project is a construction that endeavors to pay tribute to the Australians working in the Emergency Services, who fight to protect society from natural disasters and manmade catastrophes. These emergency services include the police, the fire department, ambulances, search and rescue teams, along with groups of volunteers, etc. In a symbolic and subliminal fashion, the monument embodies the collective memory of all Australians. The relationship of Australia with its natural landscape and the sacrifice of individual citizens in favor of the community are the main themes represented by this work. As in the case of all tributes, this urban intervention wishes to remain as a legacy so that future generations may

honor the sacrifice made by personnel from the emergency services.

The National Emergency Services Memorial, thanks to its special design, has become a landmark following in the tradition of this type of commemorative monument. The physical shape of the monument adapts to the slope on which it is laid, which looks out over Lake Burley Griffin.

The end result is a dialogue between the history of the surrounding buildings, the strict symmetry of Anzac Parade and the new outdoor site with its civic monuments. The architects' intention is to imbue the visitor with the complexity of human experience entailed by the extremely dangerous and risky situations in which the emergency services carry out their work. The values supported by these emergency services and the emotions felt around, during and after an emergency situation are difficult to represent in a commemorative monument.

The solution adopted by the architects was a zigzag structure measuring some 75.5 ft. in length, with each side being treated in a different way. In an entirely theatrical style, the feelings of the emergency staff are shown

with flashes of light and streaks of fire in the grass at night, creating huge shadows of the visitors. In this way, the experiences that the emergency services go through when managing a crisis or catastrophe are reflected in this monument by these same feelings being recreated with thin scraps of red material distributed over the hill and also using large shadows made by the sun and fire. Finally, the direction towards the blanket enables the visitor to experience the perception of safety provided by the Emergency Services on the actual memorial site.

This site, formed by a line of raised elements and folding forms and curves, transmits a feeling of comfort to the visitor, since as it does not involve a volume with a great deal of height, the visitor does not feel intimidated in any way.

On the eastern side of the monument, there are some words defining the values and professionalism of such personnel. On the other side there is a frieze containing a collection of images that reflect the diverse nature of tasks carried out by the emergency services, also explaining some of their experiences. Rescue scenes with helicopters and other scenes depicting the rescuers and the rescued as the protagonists of the frieze. At the bottom of the structure is a bronze projection running the whole length of the wall, which functions as a seat to rest and enjoy the views of Lake Burley Griffin.

Computer programs have been used both to create the design of the wall and the commemorative frieze and to apply innovative techniques for molding the materials. The application of these new techniques, which had never been used before in Australia, enabled the architects to create a monument on a much larger scale than would have been possible using traditional methods. The entire monument consists of three concrete panels, without any repetitions.

On the eastern side of the National Emergency Services Memorial the architects decided to inscribe rows of words on the wall defining the principles and professionalism of the personnel devoted to fighting both natural disasters and manmade catastrophes. This cement structure with folded elements creates a site for intimate solace, but at the same time it lends itself to group viewing on account of its enormous size.

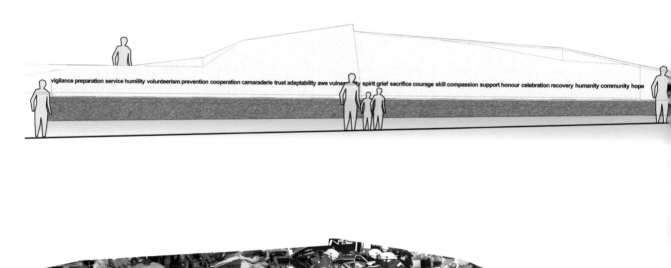

Front elevation & rear elevation

humility vulnerability pensionio cooperation camaraderie trust capability   awe vulnerability spirit grief sacrifice courage skill

Cultural Facilities

Museums
Schools & Universities
Libraries
Religious Buildings

Photo © Roger Cas

The Skyscraper Museum

New York, NY, U.S.A.   2004

ARCHITECT

SOM – Skidmore, Owings & Merrill

CLIENT

The Skyscraper Museum

PARTNERS

Roger Duffy (design); Jerome S. Gilman (consultant); Tishman Construction (building constructor); Sedlis Goldstein Group (agent); Jaros Baum & Bolles (MEP engineering); SOM Chicago (structural engineering); Pentagram (graphics); R & J Construction Corp. (general builder)

SURFACE AREA

Total area: 5,942 sq. ft.
Permanent exhibition area: 2,002 sq. ft.
Temporary exhibition area: 2,809 sq. ft.

COST

1,837,000 euros

PROGRAM

Museum devoted to the past, present, and future of skyscrapers and urban skylines

This museum is currently the only installation in the world that combines the past, present, and future of high-rise buildings and urban skylines. After spending a great many years as a nomadic institution mounting temporary exhibitions in the foyers of the historic financial district of New York, it finally found a permanent home in Battery Park City, located at Number 39, Battery Place, at the southernmost tip of Manhattan. The Skyscraper Museum occupies the ground floor of tower 38 of the Hotel Ritz-Carlton and the Condominiums. It is a logical place to put the museum, since the tower blocks in this area have witnessed more than a century of skyscraper history. Furthermore, the majestic view from the port makes it an absolute must both for the inhabitants of the city and for occasional visitors. It forms an essential part of the changing scenery downtown.

The whole site occupies a little more than 5,940 sq. ft. of exhibition space. The constructed surface area largely consists of two galleries: one devoted to the items on permanent display and the other reserved for traveling exhibitions. The precinct is completed with a bookshop and an area for administrative use by museum personnel.

The area inside is distributed by means of a series of ramps connecting the bookshop and main entrance, located at ground level, with the temporary and permanent exhibitions being located on the floor above. The display stands, which are constructed like showcases, can be moved around thanks to the wheels incorporated in the base, and this enables the area to be rearranged according to the current exhibitions and events.

The original, polished stainless steel, internal structure of the floor and ceiling creates the effect of being in an area that reaches ever upwards. It works just like a real mirror that multiplies volumes and gives the idea of a set of structures in high-rise blocks. The use of such an unconventional material for floors and ceilings provided unexpected challenges for the architects and designers. In order to maintain the purity of the mirror concept and its brightness, it was decided to seek advice from stainless steel experts, such as the Nickel Institute, and from various manufacturers in the U.S.A. and Japan. The outcome was a type of composite material

with an aluminum base shaped like a honeycomb, which would serve as reinforcement, and a stainless steel plate, which would be long-lasting and would enhance the mirror effect. In order to install the panels, the architects used a computer program, which helped ensure the panels were perfectly aligned, thereby producing a completely smooth surface that would not distort the effect of the reflected light.

Finally, this structure and internal distribution successfully bring together the desire of the architects and the institution to display photography, drawings, models, films, books, maps of the city, advertisements, and souvenirs that illustrate the mission of the museum, which is to gather, preserve and interpret the historical evolution of skyscrapers. These skyscrapers are, furthermore, explored from several angles: as designer items, as technological products, as building components, as investments in real estate, and as workplaces and residences.

This new cultural center is due not only to the architects, designers, and public authorities, but also to the donations and private funds of people interested in the creation and study of this museum site.

Perfectly aligned stainless steel and aluminum panels are used to create a mirrorlike visual effect. This gives the effect of being inside an area that reaches ever upwards, multiplying the shapes and structures in the form of a series of never-ending towers. The exhibition showcases are designed in mobile units that enable them to be repositioned and rearranged in accordance with the exhibition being staged.

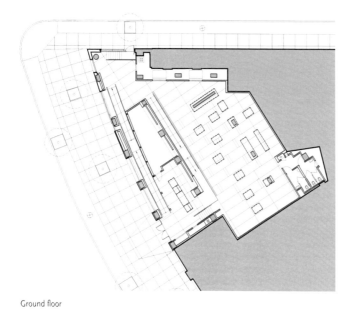

Ground floor

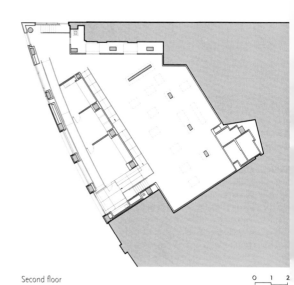

Second floor

0 1 2

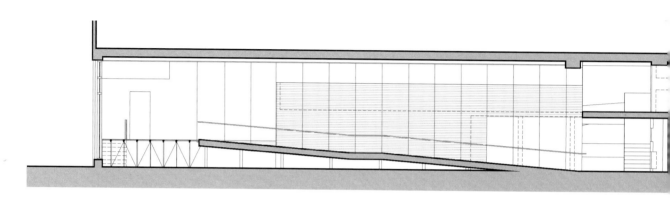

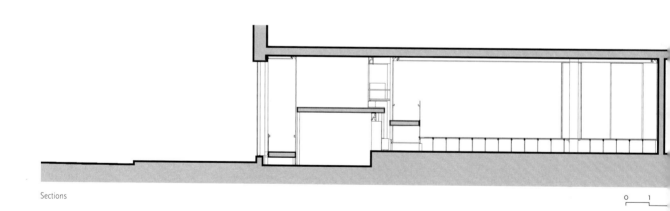

Sections

0   1

National Air and Space Museum

Chantilly, VA, U.S.A.   2003

ARCHITECT
HOK – Hellmuth, Obata & Kassabaum

CLIENT
The Smithsonian Institution

PARTNERS
Hensel Phelps Construction Company (general building contractor); HOK (mechanical and electrical engineering, interior design, landscape artist); Speigel Zamecnik & Shah (structural engineering); Law Engineering (geothermal engineering); Patton Harris Rust & Associates (civil engineering); Gage-Babcock & Associates (safety); Fisher Marantz Stone (lighting design); Constructions Consultants (cost consultant)

GENERAL SURFACE AREA
708,739 sq. ft.

COST
129,156,000 euros

PROGRAM
Museum, IMAX cinema, shops, restaurant and educational center

The National Air and Space Museum, owned by the prestigious Smithsonian Institution, dated back to the 1960s and was in need of extension. The existing museum could only house a small part of the whole collection and it was no longer possible to show all the material held in storage. The same architects that had designed the original museum were commissioned to design its new transformation. The aim was to convert the old center into a magnificent museum housing the historic collection of aircraft and spacecraft, and, at the same time, provide new facilities for the exhibition and conservation of the various exhibits. The institution was also interested in having a large area available for collecting private donations, while generating income at the same time. This money is earmarked for the preservation and protection of the exhibits from the adverse effects of the environment, such as fluctuations in temperature, humidity, light, etc.

The project is located at Dulles International Airport and, therefore, the architects drew their inspiration for the interior design from an airport terminal, with the shape and detail following the aeronautical tradition that the museum pays homage to. Thus, the museum was designed to simulate the basic structure of an airport: the areas were divided into a groundside area and an airside zone, and included a lobby, an IMAX film theater, and an iconic control tower. Groundside is designed on a human scale, and this is where the entrance to the museum, the souvenir shop, a visitors' restaurant, an educational center, the personnel administration offices, the film theatre and observation tower are all located. The area is lit up by direct sunlight, thereby greeting the visitors in symbolic fashion. The airside area holds the museum's main hangars, with huge doors allowing for the passage of airplanes in and out of the hangars. The floors are also prepared to take the weight of a launchpad, for instance. These hangars correspond respectively to the main exhibition hall, the zone for outer space, the restaurant and catering facilities, and the warehouses for storing the various artifacts.

The spectacular nature of the museum is particularly apparent in the main hangar. The architects wanted to display a simulation of

the sky, by creating high ceilings painted in the clear colors that are typical of the sky, lit up solely with artificial light. In the hangar there are no corners, and the sun hardly sheds any light inside, and even then, only indirectly. The show continues with the sight of a plane hanging from the roof, which can be approached by the visitors via raised walkways that pass close by. This enables them to experience the feeling of ascending in parallel with the plane, and also allows them to take a detailed look at the exhibits from close up. The other planes are arranged at different heights, enabling them to be seen from various different angles.

Most of the elements forming part of the museum are covered in bright, bluish aluminum panels. Ceramic tiles with a metallic appearance are also used for facings and evoke materials used in the construction of space objects. The outer appearance of the facade is obviously smooth, with areas that are glazed with straight, rectangular-shaped panes of glass.

The museum is also known as the Udvar-Hazy Center, in honor of the founder and general manager of the International Lease Finance Corporation, Steven F. Udvar-Hazy, who donated $65 million towards its construction. Because the Smithsonian Institution did not wish to charge an admission fee, great emphasis was placed on gathering funds for its construction. For this reason, HOK designed and constructed the project in stages, as funds were raised from donations. Since the time of its opening to the public, which coincided with the centenary of the first powered flight, the number of visitors has risen steadily. Today, it is one of the most popular museums in the world.

The main hangar is located airside, where the majority of planes in the collection are on display. The architects designed a series of raised walkways in order for the artifacts to be viewed from all angles and also in greater detail. The high ceilings in the hangars make it possible for artificial lighting to be installed, with indirect sunlight only. This lighting is also a result of the intention to protect the artifacts from the effects of the environment, which accelerates deterioration.

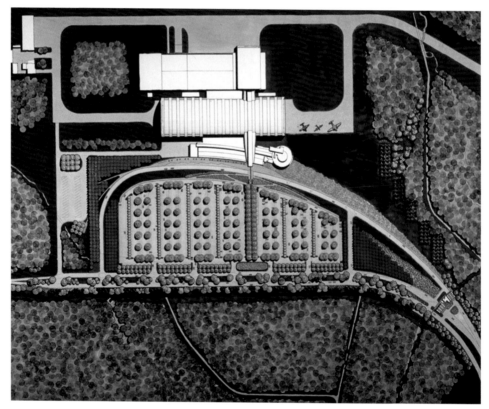

Location plan

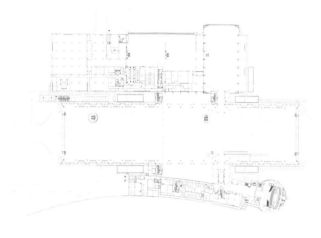

First floor

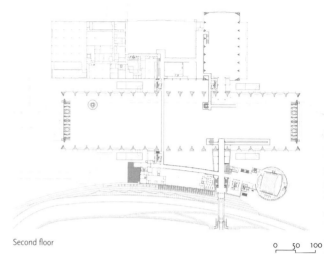

Second floor

0   50   100

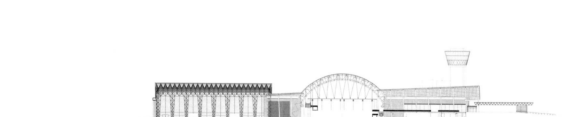

Cross section

0   20   40

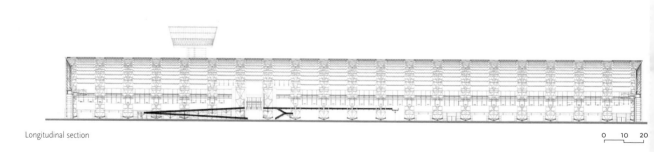

Longitudinal section

0   10   20

Photo © Brígida González, Christian Richter

Mercedes-Benz Museum

Stuttgart, Germany   2006

ARCHITECT
UNStudio

CLIENT
DCI – DaimlerChrysler Immobilien

PARTNERS
*DCI – DaimlerChrysler Immobilien
(constructors); Prof. H. G. Merz (museum
design)*

CONSTRUCTED SURFACE AREA
Height: 156 ft.
Floors: nine
Total surface area: 570,487 sq. ft.
Ground plan surface area: 51,667 sq. ft.
Exhibition surface area: 177,605 sq. ft.
Interior volumetric surface: 7,416,080 cu. ft.

COST
150 million euros

PROGRAM
*New museum to house the historical Mercedes-
Benz automobile collection*

The new Mercedes-Benz museum was inaugurated on May 19, 2006 in Stuttgart. This museum is located close to the B14 motorway at the entrance to the city and covers 570,487 sq. ft. of urban space for the 120-year history of the automobile, composed of 160 cars and 1,500 unique pieces on display in a two-hour long exhibition. The architectural space is primarily the nine-story museum building with its 177,605 sq. ft. exhibition space, projected by the studio of Dutch architects, UN Studio. With various factors against them, such as the complex and innovative character of the museum and the limited time to design, plan and carry out the project (just two and a half years), the result came from an intense collaborative effort between the client DaimlerChrysler Immobilien (DCI), engineers, meteorology experts, interior designers, urban architects, and exhibition designers. The basic principles of Mercedes-Benz are its originality, the impulse to conceive and create new forms of mobility, from the invention of the car to a futuristic vision of a world without traffic accidents.

As an annex to the exhibition, there are diverse spaces like the museum shop, a restaurant, offices, and a large reception area, as well as the urbanization of the surrounding landscape that must accommodate 450,000 visitors a year.

The main building attempts to link tradition by exhibiting the history of this car company, with modernity using a spiral-shaped futuristic design, evoking the double outline of DNA that holds a human's genetic inheritance. Following the same system of symbols, the museum aims to keep the genetic inheritance of these unique gems from Mercedes-Benz. This architecture was so complex it required the help of the latest computer technology, which allowed the digital control of the geometry in all aspects of the building.

On arriving at the museum, the visitor is faced with a spectacular 138-ft.-high atrium, where elevators take you up to the top floor of the building. This is where the two routes start that take visitors around the collection, conceived as a journey through time and through the different products. The lifts are like closed capsules with a large slit at eye level, through which the visitor can see images of the project's history. The two

ramps twist in a descending spiral; on one route, we find the first link of the chain, the so-called *Legent* (Legends) hall comprised of seven rooms that tell the chronological tale of the company's history and are artificially lit like theatrical spaces. In the second route we find five independent collections, representing a variety of products from the brand without making any temporal distinction, and surrounded by enormous panoramic windows. The two tours cross constantly, imitating the interweaving filaments of DNA and making it possible for the visitors to change their route when they like. Both ramps end in a steeply sloping curve where visitors can admire the legend of this brand in its purest form, the races and the records. The tour finally ends in the technical fascination, where we see the work of present-day engineers, together with the future that awaits us.

The materials used outside for the facade are aluminum panels and large windows made from 1,800 triangular sheets of glass taking full advantage of the natural light and thereby representing significant energy savings. It is no coincidence that aluminum and glass have been used for the facade; the architects took them from the materials used for the car exteriors. In the same way, the exterior architectural structure, based on the shape of a clover consisting of three overlapping circles whose center forms the atrium, seems to pay homage to the knot of nearby roads. The elegant ramps of different heights are similar to the lanes of a racetrack.

The museum's interior houses seven exhibition rooms that look back through the 120-year history of Mercedes-Benz. The double tour throughout the nine floors of technical and sporting achievements is done through ramps that descend around a central atrium.

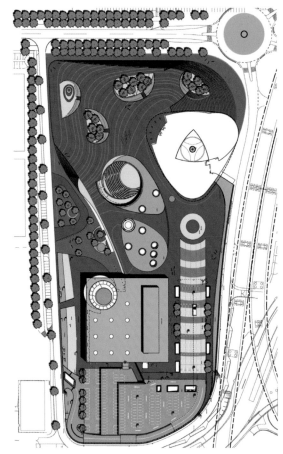

Location plan

The building, which seems to defy gravity and float above the ground, weighs 110,000 tons. The materials used on the exterior facade are aluminum sheets and large windows formed from 1,800 triangular sheets of glass of different sizes that allow natural light to enter from outside.

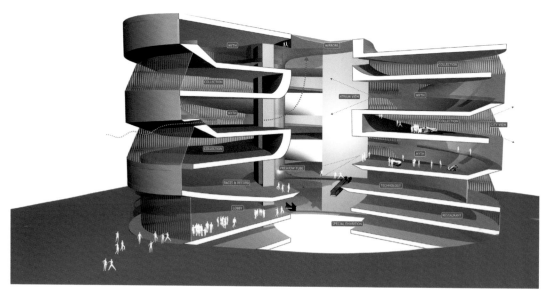

Render

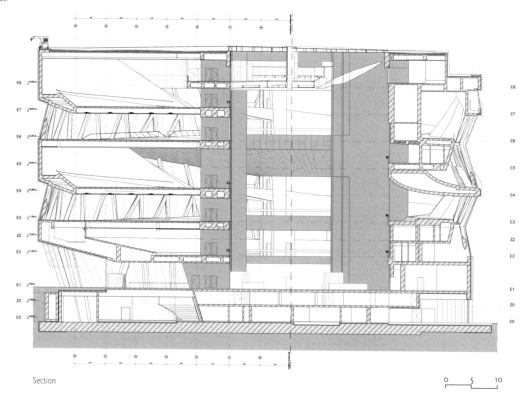

Section

0   5   10

Photo © Pep Escod

Musée du Quai Branly

Paris, France   2006

ARCHITECT
Ateliers Jean Nouvel

CLIENT
Etablissement Public du Musée du Quai Branly

PARTNERS
Ingerop (structure); OTH (fluid mechanics); Acanthe (landscape design); AIK (lighting design); Patrick Blanc (plant wall designer); Arcora (facade); GEC Ingénierie (finishings); Observatoire Nff1 (lighting); Avel Acoustique (acoustics); Duck's (scenography); Caso & Cie (security)

AREA
Overall area of complex: 823,400 sq. ft.
Built area: 437,700 sq. ft.

COST
204 million euros

PROGRAM
Museum, cultural center, education and research center, bookstore, media library, auditorium, screening room, store, garden, and parking

This museum was designed to display and house works of art from little-known non-Western cultures, as well as to promote the research and teaching of these art forms. The collections come from the Laboratory of Ethnology of the Museum of Mankind and the former African and Oceanic Arts museum, and they comprise 300,000 items from Africa, America, Asia, and Oceania spread over various buildings with a total area of 430,600 sq. ft. designed by this prestigious team of local architects. It is undoubtedly an architectural as well as a historical phenomenon; this impressive setting houses one of the biggest art collections in the world, putting them on an equal footing with the rest of the world's art works, despite their being unknown art forms that were not appreciated until very recently.

There was an international call for tenders in January 1999; the world's most prestigious architects submitted bids, and the winning bid came from the Jean Nouvel team of architects. The project consisted of an idea of architecture that respected the environment, both in the use of nonaggressive materials and with regard to the urban land-scape of the heart of Paris. The museum complex of four buildings is very near the Eiffel Tower, right in the heart of Paris. For the building of the complex, the architects took into account functionality and integrating the building into the urban and natural surroundings. The main building of the complex is made of a 660 ft. long glassed-in and silk-screened walkway that runs over a 4.5-acre garden raised on large pillars. The garden boasts 180 trees, each over 50 ft. high, that hide this walkway. An access ramp leads to an area measuring 70,000 sq. ft. for permanent exhibitions; for temporary exhibitions, 27,000 sq. ft. have been set aside. Grays, reds, browns, blacks, and navy blues predominate on the outside of this building. A 500-seat auditorium, a 120-seat screening room, a media library with 12,000 reference books, a bookstore, and finally the panoramic restaurant and bar make up the rest of the museum.

The museum's interior layout is designed as if it were an open platform that opens the visitor's eyes and mind to these new art forms. The spiral access ramp leads to the collections platform and a fictitious map

represents an imaginary archipelago made up of the various cultural groups. On one side of the main walkway are all the objects related to Asia and Africa, and on the other side, those of Oceania and the Americas. This seamless route enables visitors to stop at the major thematic items: costumes from Asia, musical instruments and textiles from Africa, masks from Oceania, and finally religious objects from the Americas. In addition to the items on display, there are more than a hundred audio-visual installations that are informative and raise the visitor's awareness. The soft spotlighting plays with shadows, and the colors chosen for the interior are warm and intense, designed to absorb the light. In the central part, above the platform, there is a hanging gallery for visitors to meditate, extend their visit, and delve a little deeper into the themes that have made the most impression on them. Users can have fun interacting with the encyclopedia programs installed here. There are also Braille texts, tactile bas-reliefs, touchscreens, and so on, that enable visitors to relate to the space around them.

This place has been designed as a leisure center for cultural exchanges and as an assembly of different civilizations; theater, dance and music events are scheduled every year. The aim for the museum is to become a symbol of peace and brotherhood between peoples.

The building is characterized by a mixture of styles that blend with nature, as this was the main objective of the design. The materials used, such as cement and glass panels, integrate perfectly with the natural wood of the vegetation. The facades of the administration buildings are hidden behind a thick curtain of climbing plants.

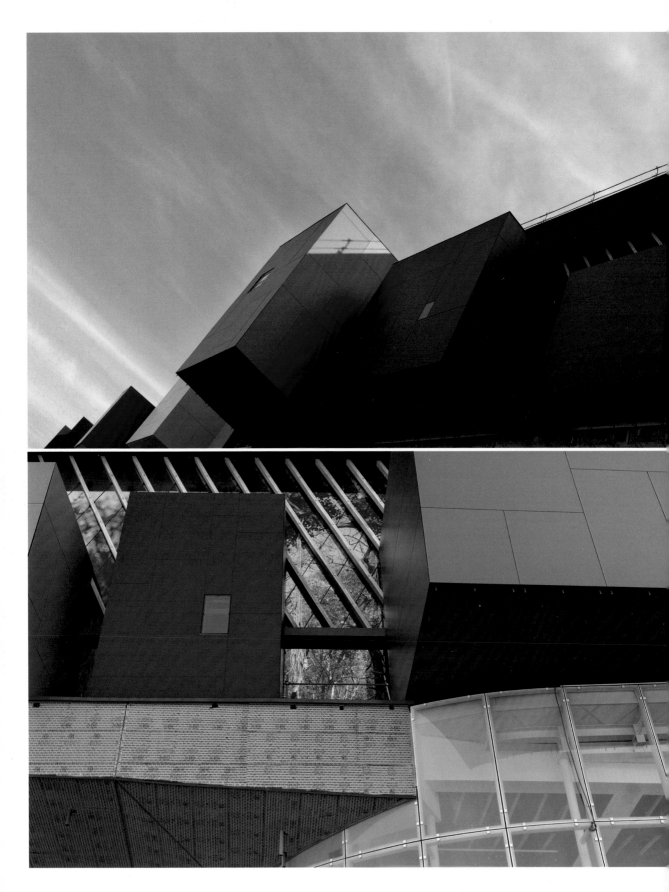

The architects decided that the four buildings making up the Quai Branly museum would each be different. The main building is a walkway in the shape of a vast curved glass wall, supported on pillars. At the top, there is a horizontal line of boxes painted in shades of terracotta, purple, and ochre. Another striking building is the row of curved lines constructed with glass panels designed to house temporary exhibitions.

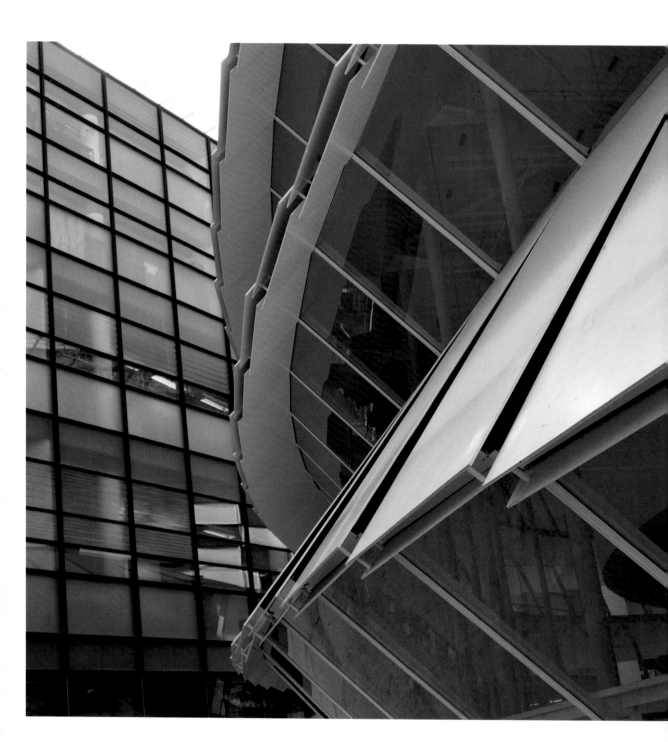

Photo © Bitter Bre

Extension to the Denver Art Museum

Denver, CO, U.S.A.   2006

ARCHITECT
Studio Daniel Libeskind

CLIENT
City of Denver and the Denver Art Museum

PARTNERS
Davis Partnership Architects (associate architects); Stefan Blach, Arne Emerson, Guadalupe Cantu, Robert Claiborne (project architects); Arup (structural engineering)

AREA
146,000 sq. ft.

COST
58,500,000 euros

PROGRAM
New extension to the Denver Art Museum, store, café and theater

The Denver Art Museum extension has been added onto the existing museum, designed in 1971 by the Italian architect, Gio Ponti. This new structure has been named after Frederic C. Hamilton and is the result of painstaking work by the team of architects, the director, the curators, staff, and the state. Although belonging to the same institution, the two museums are treated architecturally as two separate buildings linked by a glassed-in steel bridge built on this extension. It houses the collection of Modern and Contemporary American Art, as well as African Art and Design and Oceanic and Western Art. The extension was designed to revitalize this cultural center in Denver and to become, in a short space of time, an icon that would define it and mark it apart from other cities. The intention is to attract a large number of visitors, locals, and outsiders alike.

The building has become the main entrance to the complex and inside is a passageway that leads to the stores, cafeteria and theatre. This link has a similar design to the previously existing museum, the civic center and the public library, in both function and

aspect. It is thus a joint link with the city center and the civic center, establishing a strong connection with the city's golden triangle. In short, the building is treated not as a separate building but as a component of a composition of public spaces, monuments and gateways into this part of the city that is constantly expanding.

With this spectacular facade, the team of architects aimed to reflect the growing development of the city, as well as its inspiration from the magnificent surrounding landscape, dominated by spectacular views of the Rocky Mountains. This gives rise to a dialogue between a brave construction project and a romantic landscape, resulting in a space that is unique in the world. The choice of materials for this new building was governed by a desire to reflect the connection between tradition and modernity. Thus the local stone, granite, was used, together with new materials that are typical of 21st century architecture, such as titanium. The result is an angular structure consisting of 2,700 tons of steel, 3,100 steel girders and 468,202 cu. ft. of cement, covered with 9,000 titanium and granite panels. The

building projects towards the north, and as it extends in that direction, the number of floors rises from two to four. Its original facade reminds one of the folds in a piece of Japanese origami, characterized by the multiple polygonal right angle features in granite and titanium. These right-angled elements are reminiscent of the nearby mountain peaks. Once again, as is common in the new architecture of this century, the assistance of computer software has been essential for the construction.

Access to the museum is via the 120 ft. high Pomar Grand Atrium, which has the same slanting walls in the interior as the exterior facade. A broad staircase on one of the lateral walls leads to the exhibition galleries and a passageway to the 280-seat theater. This wing also contains souvenir stores and a cafeteria for visitors to take a breather. Next, the visitor crosses the bridge that links the two museums. This bridge leads to the Duncan Pavil-

ion, with an area of 20,677 sq. ft., whose glazed facade affords a view of the natural landscape outside. With this new building, three new exhibition spaces have been created: on the first floor, the Anschutz Gallery and the Gallagher Family Gallery, given over to temporary exhibitions, and on the second floor, the Martin & McCormick Gallery.

The constantly changing light, the atmospheric effects and Denver's own typical climate changes posed a big challenge in the construction of the building. The facade changes tones and appearance depending on the light from the sun and the visitor's angle of vision. The main architectural feature is its integration and respect for the general public rather than a reflection of a spectacular interior or exterior. The building is a clear example of the urban dialogue between architecture and the public, which reflects the vitality and constant growth of this American city.

The 146,000 sq. ft. of area, the 468,202 cu. ft. of cement, the 2,700 tons of steel, 3,100 steel girders, and 9,000 titanium and granite panels are the most striking features of this new Denver Art Museum extension. As well as this innovative museum, the architects have designed the adjoining plaza and an apartment complex that is set to draw a large public.

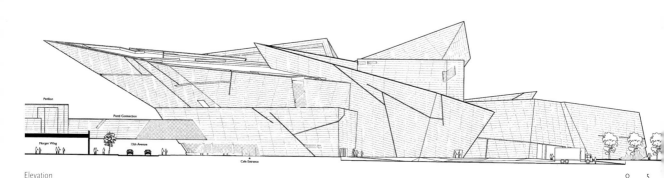

Elevation

0   5

The main inspiration for the creation of this museum complex was the vitality and development of this American city, as well as the romantic landscape provided by the spectacular views of the Rocky Mountains. The architectural geometry, in folded, right-angled rectangular creases is reminiscent of Japanese origami structures.

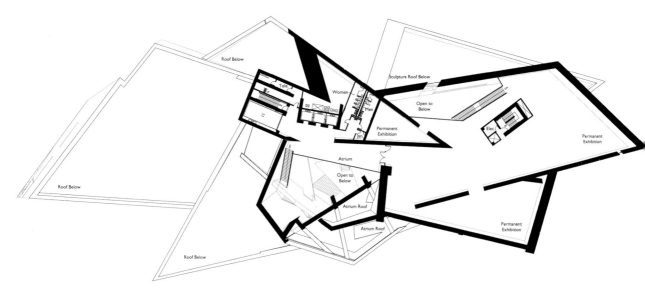

Ground floor

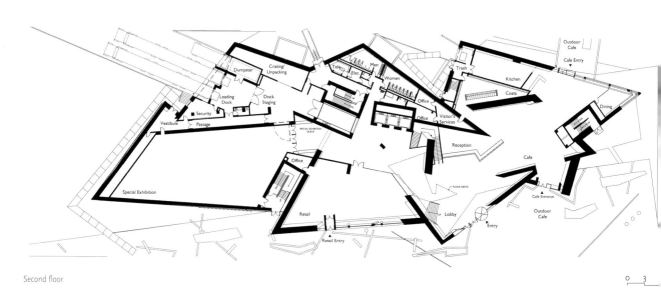

Second floor

0   3

Photo © Andy Rya

MIT Stata Center

Cambridge, MA, U.S.A.   2004

ARCHITECT
Gehry Partners

CLIENT
Massachusetts Institute of Technology

PARTNERS
Nancy Joyce (project manager); Gehry Partners (architectural design); Cannon Design (associate architect); Olin Partnership (landscape architecture); R. G. Vanderweil Engineers (MEP engineering); John A. Martin & Associates (structural engineering); Skanska U.S.A. Building (construction manager)

AREA
721,200 sq. ft.

COST
234 million euros

PROGRAM
Installations for the Computer Science and Artificial Intelligence Laboratory, the Laboratory for Information and Decision Systems, and the Department of Linguistics and Philosophy. Also, lecture rooms, auditoria, social areas, gymnasium, day-care center, and underground garage

The new Ray and Maria Stata center for Computer Science, Information, and Intelligence at the Massachusetts Institute of Technology (MIT) was built in honor of the founder of Analog Devices Inc. and his wife, who donated $25 million towards its construction. It was built to replace the old building that stood on 2.8 acres. That building was erected hastily during World War II and was known less for architecture than for housing the activities of the foremost scientists of the 20th century. It was an office block built of gray concrete. Known as Building 20, it was important at the time because of the scientific breakthroughs, such as radar, that were made inside it.

The university authorities wanted the exterior design to show in a constructive manner the work that was to be done inside. The architects were quick to seize the idea and decided to employ innovative building concepts, the result being just one more example of their vast creative talent. Their solution consisted of creating different volumes (cubes, cones, and towers) using various materials (steel, aluminum, and brick) and colors (silver, yellow, shades of brown) that would seamlessly blend with each other. There are broken lines, deliberately asymmetrical forms, as well as angular and geometric shapes that seem to defy the force of gravity.

Inside, this multiplicity is transposed into a maze of vestibules, ramps, and galleries that favor discussion and personal relationships, as well as interaction between the occupants to stimulate a higher level of performance.

Interior distribution is by means of a long corridor that connects the two main towers and leads to the spaces devoted to teaching, the lecture rooms, the cafeteria, and so on. One level up from the corridor are the patio and dining area for the center's occupants. One of the main towers is given over to research activities and the other to teaching and public-access activities. The two towers are identical in structure and are six stories high. On the ground floor are the auditorium and the pub, with the original floor of Building 20. In addition to the two main towers, there is a circular robotics laboratory and a yellow circular building for seminars. The building with the most sloping facade houses a two-level underground parking garage, with space for 700 cars. At ground level

there is also a day-care center for 65 children and other spaces for services.

The magnitude of various construction materials used shows the architectural complexity of the project: 12,800 aluminum panels weighing 1,300 tons; 120,000 tons of concrete for the foundations and bases; 1 million bricks and 71,000 sq. ft. of glass.

As is common with the most recent of contemporary buildings, it has installations designed for the rational use of resources thanks to optimum use of natural light and the use of recycled rainwater. The interior facades have large windows that let in natural light; this removes the need for artificial light during the day. A collection system enables rainwater to be used for bathrooms.

There have been many comments on the overall appearance of the MIT Stata facade. Frank O. Gehry said, tongue in cheek, that "it looks like a party of drunken robots." Researchers have also joked about its unusual appearance: "We've already had one earthquake in the Stata Center, so we don't have to worry about any more." Other comments, based on the multiple shapes and color scheme of the building, refer to Disney cartoons. In any event, the new MIT concept is the product of deep thought by the architect, who has considered future users of the center, their needs, and their work areas. This has given rise to a space where the mind is free, the walls are moveable, and the rooms can be laid out depending on users' requirements.

The multiple volumes—cubes, cones and towers—that make up this research and development center are constructed with malleable materials, such as steel, bricks, aluminum, and glass. As well as providing varied textures, they give the building a seamlessly varied color scheme.

The architects have designed interior spaces where natural light is the principal element. The walls can be moved so that different layouts can be achieved depending on the requirements of the various services. The complexity of the construction is remarkable for its originality in combining flat, angular surfaces and undulating, curved volumes.

Seattle Central Library

Seattle, WA, U.S.A.   2004

ARCHITECT
*OMA – Office for Metropolitan Architecture,
LMN Architects*

CLIENT
The Seattle Public Library

PARTNERS
*Arup, Magnusson Klemencic Associates
(engineering); Michael Yantis Associates
(acoustics); Mc Guire Associates (ADA); Ann
Hamilton, Gary Hill, Tony Oursler (artists);
OMA, LMN, Maarten van Severen (interior
design); Jones & Jones (landscaping); Kugler
Tillotson Associates (lighting)*

SURFACE AREA
412,000 sq. ft.

COST
131,359,000 euros

PROGRAM
*Central library, reading room, Book Spiral,
mixing chamber, meeting platforms, lounge,
administration department, children's
collection, auditorium and carpark*

In 1999 the Dutch architectural firm OMA and LMN Architects were awarded the tender for the central public library in Seattle. It is considered to be one of the last architectural projects addressed to the general public and one in which they might select the most attractive project. It was the citizens themselves that tilted the balance in favor of the winning architectural design. In spite of the advent of the so-called digital age, people still use books printed on paper. This was the conclusion reached by both clients and architects in designing the new library, following a meticulous study of American and European libraries. Reflecting such cultural and social development, it was decided that the library should invite the public to enter and form part of its world. It was suggested that the library should be redefined as an institution not solely devoted to the book, but as a mine of information in which all potential means of communication, both old and new, are presented in a legible way and on an equal footing. The idea is that the library should not seem threatened by the newly emerging technologies, but should rather provide shelter and take them into its

fold. In an age where information can be consulted from anywhere in the world and can be issued by any medium, simultaneity on the part of all the media mean that the library will take on a vital role.

Contemporary libraries have become and are conceived to be the very creation of generic spaces in which almost any activity can take place: reading for children, screen projections, meetings to discuss various topics, performances, etc. The important thing where architects are concerned is the public space and the relationships that can be established there by the visitors or users. The outcome of such challenging reflection is a single building with a single volume, multiplied by the use of various platforms and with a splendid facade made of glass and steel. 9,994 pieces of glass were used for the outside and 4,644 tons of steel for the structure. Since there were an extremely wide variety of forms, empty spaces of differing heights were created. The design is also original in its use of vibrant colors in some of the rooms, in the intervention of graphic artists on the floors and walls, and finally, in the automatic mechanisms for the distribution of books.

The architects split the project into two areas: stable areas, which corresponded to more traditional uses, and unstable areas, of uncertain use. The first area is divided into five sections arranged in various dimensions and densities, so as to get the most out of the space available. Here we find the administrative departments and offices, a structure in the form of a spiral where the books are kept, along with conference rooms, staff rooms and parking areas. These areas are independent and each has their own mechanical and structural systems. In the intermediate areas between the different levels are the transit zones where the aim is to give the user information. It is in this aspect that there is the greatest amount of interaction between visitors and it is where the game-like effect sought by the architects comes into play. There are five unstable areas: the reading room, the mixing chamber where the librarians look up information, the lounge, the children's reading room, and the multilingual sections. Each of these is reserved for different, specific tasks but they are not completely independent. Instead, there is a certain degree of flexibility. This internal structure is what gives the building its dynamic nature and organic appearance. This is also the case with respect to the outside of the building, where the glass and steel structure also attempts to disassociate itself from conventional mores.

The Spiral Book was built to house over 1.4 million books, placed on a belt climbing up four floors. This frees the librarians mechanically from the need to handle great volumes of material. In the mixing chamber, the librarians are there to advise the user. All this technology in the central classification and registration system means that it takes no longer than 10 minutes to find the item requested by the user. The interior design is also original, since organic pictures and gigantic typographic works have been fixed to the walls as decoration.

Since it opened to the public, the new library has become the new icon of the city of Seattle, and is one of the most popular architectural sites visited by the tourists that come to this city.

In this library, the most striking architectural element, visually speaking, is its facade. Complicated to build, it is formed by a structural framework of steel and a skin made of 9,994 triangular pieces of glass. This glazed external structure allows the interior to be bathed in direct sunlight, thereby creating an original geometric design reflected on the floor of the various rooms.

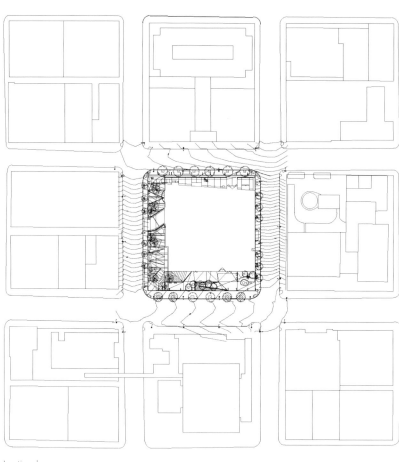

Location plan

The new central library in Seattle was not conceived as a place to store thousands of books, but rather as a building in which visitors and users could interact among themselves and with new technologies. The building was designed to defend public property and in addition, over the years, it has become a new icon in this city.

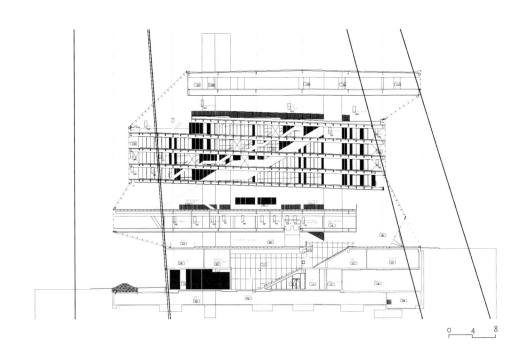

0   4   8

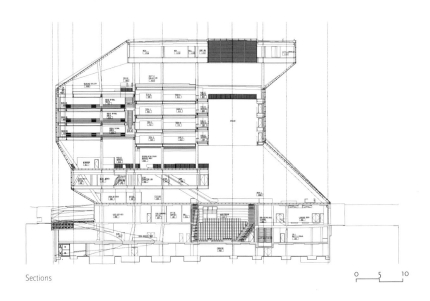

Sections

0   5   10

Photo © Pep Escod

Saint François de Molitor Church

Paris, France   2005

ARCHITECT
Corinne Callies, Jean-Marie Duthilleul/AREP

CLIENT
Association Diocésaine de Paris

PARTNERS
*Michel Desvigne (landscaping); iGuzzini,
Denis Perrin (lighting); Sorit Investissement
(developer); Philippe Talbot et Associés, Eric
Bordelet (site director); AREP (acoustics);
Bethac (plumbing); Kephen Ingénierie
(concrete structures)*

AREA
*Area: 14,960 sq. ft.
Area of church: 4,950 sq. ft.*

PROGRAM
Church and parish hall to seat 420 parishioners

March 18, 2005 saw the consecration of this new church, which replaced a small parish church that had been built in 1941. The new site is 44 Rue Molitor in Paris. The Archbishop of Paris decided to build a new church to replace the original, as it was small and built with materials that were unsafe for worshippers. After a good many technical studies conducted to prevent total demolition, it was decided to rebuild the old chapel almost from scratch. This renovation also embodied the acts of a united and coordinated community.

Its location all along the street calls to mind the Bible in that it establishes a relationship between the city (the image of Jerusalem) and the garden (the image of Eden). As in the Bible, this relationship begins in the Garden of Eden and ends in the Heavenly City. Both the city and the garden are also two of the most important places in the life of St. Francis of Assisi. It is therefore understandable that the community should gather around the Eucharistic table between these two spaces, and on this axis.

The building is a large area formed by white marble panels against translucent glass, which filters the light entering the interior rooms from the south. The choice of this type of marble was no coincidence, as the architects wanted the color scheme to blend in with the neighboring buildings while at the same time echoing the beauty and importance of the sacred nature of the site. The translucent marble enables this volume to be transformed at night into an impressive beacon of light.

At first sight, the exterior of the building gives no clue as to its true function, but there are two signs that show that a church is to be found therein: the three massive wooden doors opening onto the portico and the bell tower flanking the west side of the building. These entrance and exit doors face south, towards the city. The portico is the first space one comes to when entering the church. The atmosphere here is quiet and shaded, to indicate that it is a transitional space between the bustle of the street and the whispered prayers of a sacred place. Through a large glass panel, facing the entrance, one can see an exotic garden comprising Japanese maples and a small stretch of water. This small pond is surrounded by

beds of grasses that lend spectacular beauty to the setting. The garden is the representation of nature in its purest state, the place where St. Francis prayed among his "brother and sister creatures." Just before the glass panel is a large cross that marks the final part of the entrance axis. This cross, situated like a tree on a path, interacts with those in the garden. It is a radiant cross lit up by the light coming through the glass from the south. In front of the cross, on the same axis, is the pulpit, the lectern, where the word is proclaimed through the reading of the Holy Scriptures.

On the opposite side of the pulpit, near the entrance alongside the Lady Chapel, is the large baptismal font. It is placed near the entrance expressly so as to welcome the newly baptized to the community. Two side galleries extend the enveloping movement of the congregation upwards around the altar, thereby providing seating for 420 wor-

shippers. Around the altar, the floor slopes downwards, like the bottom of a boat or a pair of cupped hands gathering water from a spring. The nave is the evangelical symbol of the church. Around it there are two curved walls made of the golden stone typical of Paris, enclosing the congregation. The ambulatory and galleries are in an almond shape, in line with the curved structure that characterizes the interior of the building.

It is all covered with a horizontal box-shaped structure, partly dominated by the parish properties, partly protected by glass, beneath which are some timber boards with slight gaps between them that enables the light to pass through and illuminate the altar. To the west there are three doors leading into the small chapel. It is the cave representing the beginning and end of Christ's earthly life, where a worshipper can go at any time of the day to pray and meet the community.

The architects have created a space full of mystery, in the very heart of Paris, and calm, with a simple volume and timeless materials: stone, wood, and glass. There are many features that evoke the Bible and the Church, such as the layout of the sunken floor, like the bottom of a boat, the evangelical symbol of the Church.

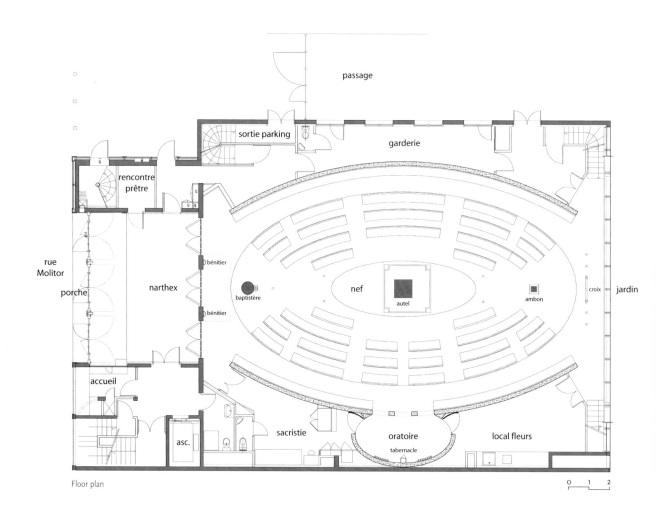

Floor plan

In this sacred place the main light comes in through the large glass panel situated on the south axis of the church. This glass wall affords a permanent view of the garden, made up of Japanese maples and grasses. At night, artificial lights reproduce the same atmosphere of peace and calm that the place gives off in daylight.

Leisure Facilities

Auditoriums
Theaters & Cinemas
Sports Facilities
Bars & Discotheques
Shopping Malls
Stores & Showrooms
Restaurants

Photo © Auditorio de Tenerife, José Ramón Ol

Tenerife Auditorium

Tenerife, Spain   2003

ARCHITECT
Santiago Calatrava

CLIENT
Cabildo Insular de Tenerife

PARTNERS
*UTE between Acciona and Dragados
(constructors); Ingeniería Aguilera
(engineering); Alfonso García Sanchermes
and BBM Müller (acoustics); Chemtrol (Stage),
CYMI (electrical installations)*

CONSTRUCTED SURFACE AREA
*General surface area: 172,000 sq. ft.
Ground plan surface area: 67,800 sq. ft.
Site: 142,000 sq. ft.*

COST
74 million euros

PROGRAM
*Auditorium for music, opera, theatre, dance,
meetings, and conferences*

The Tenerife Auditorium is located in the coastal area of Cabo Llanos, making it the most important recreational space in Tenerife's Santa Cruz. This building opens the city to the sea and the island's landscapes, characterized by the contrast between a more avant-garde, contemporary design and the typically colorful local architecture. The space revives the area next to the sea as a transitional element between land and sea and creates an urban landmark within the city. When seen from above, it has the shape of an eye, where the building is the pupil and the surrounding spaces the eyeball. The white part of the eye is a wide, open surface area, which plays host to the 172,000 sq. ft. set of public squares made from slabs of stone from the island, which contrast with the whiteness of the building. The appearance of the auditorium, beforehand, is that of a magnificent dynamic sculpture more than a merely functional construction, as is normally typical from architect Santiago Calatrava. This sensation is reinforced by the spaces and, thanks to the ceilings and patterns of natural light, offers the sensation of walking through a mobile, futuristic sculpture.

The most striking and characteristic elements of the Tenerife Auditorium are the expressive shapes of the ceilings. The Wing, a large, exterior concrete feature, was built as a triangular protecting roof which emerges from the back part of the Auditorium, leans on the vertex of the nut and reaches a height of 190 feet, reducing its width and side. It looks as if the Wing covers almost the entire length of the building. The structure seems to defy the laws of gravity due to its colossal size and daring shape. This structural and geometric rigor carries great expression and artistic intention, making the artistic character of the activities inside transcend to the outside. The white ceramic *trencadís* finish allows it to be seen from a distance and, in turn, reflects the luminosity of the city. Three cylindrical sheets of concrete in the shape of lateral arches frame the entrances to the building, contrasting with the central piece. Resting on these elements are two lateral, cone-shaped shells of the same material, which, like candles, line the container of the Auditorium. The load of these large shells is transmitted to the foundations through the lateral arches.

The symphony hall, with a capacity of 1,600 people, is the building's generating element both formally and structurally. Located inside the organically curved cone, it is surrounded by the two lateral conical surfaces and, being adjacent to the main hall, this vestibule acts as an acoustic softener to the noise outside, as well as a waiting room. The stage of the main hall is 53 ft. deep and 56 ft. wide, with three independent platforms; two for the orchestra and one to store stage machinery.

The chamber hall accommodates up to 432 people and is situated diametrically opposite the main hall, taking advantage of the site's geometry. The roof stands out artistically, formed from longitudinal lobes finished in arris and with illuminated gaps in the sides. It is equipped to host all kinds of activity thanks to its marvelous acoustics, excellent visibility, and comfort. Between the chamber hall and the passageway is a hall, which acts as an acoustic softener and practically wraps around the entire chamber hall. There are also two complementary buildings, the parking lot and a space for offices and storage.

This architectural piece, despite appearing homogenous from afar, can be appreciated from many different perspectives. At night a visual effect is produced in the auditorium's tiles reflecting the city and the sea on several light planes.

The hall, with a surface area of 12,600 sq. ft., distributes the spectators that come to the events in the Chamber Hall and Symphonic Hall (see the following page). It is closed on both sides by two large doors made of glass and wood with a metal structure, which open and close automatically.

Photo © Paul Czitrom Baus, Werner Huthma[...]

Gota de Plata Auditorium Theater

Pachuca, Mexico   2005

ARCHITECT
Jaime Varon, Abraham Metta, Álex Metta/Migdal Arquitectos

CLIENT
Government of the state of Hidalgo, Mexico

PARTNERS
ITISA – Impulsora Tlaxcalteca de Industrias (structure and principal contractor); CTC Civil Engineers; AKF Engineers (electromechanical installations design); Luz y Forma (lighting and theatre mechanics design); Miguel Kuri Gehring (aluminium and glass design); Eduardo Saad Eljure, Omar Saad (isoptic and acoustic design); Laboratorios Tlalli (floor mechanism)

AREA
*Total construction area: 150,700 sq. ft.
Area: 75,350 sq. ft.*

PROGRAM
Culture auditorium in the David Ben Gurion complex

This theater-auditorium is situated in the city of Pachuca del Soto, the capital of the state of Hidalgo, 60 miles north of Mexico City. It is historically famous for mineral prospecting, particularly silver, making it one of the foremost mining centers in the country. Today, it is also a busy commercial and cultural center, with a wide variety of architectural styles.

The structure is part of the David Ben Gurion Culture and Recreation Complex, a 62-acre complex situated in the Zona Plateada. This culture and services complex was built thanks to public bodies and private developers who set up a partnership for a cultural community center for the inhabitants of Pachuca. A good many architects, builders, and even artists took part in the project. The nerve centre of the complex is a large elongated plaza, where a local artist, Byron Gálvez, designed a 260-by-1,300 ft. mural. The mosaic is made of small bright-colored tiles that form a 338,000 sq. ft. image. Around this area other amenities were built such as the Museum of Contemporary Art, Science and Technology Museum, Audiorama, Sculpture Park, Central Library, Convention Center, and finally a five-star hotel.

When the architects were told where the theatre was to be situated, they designed a building that would reflect the plaza's mural while acting as a vantage point for the work, so that visitors to the complex would feel visually attracted by this theater-plaza combination. The roof structure, at a height of 82 ft., managed to establish this two-way exchange. It acts like a mirror formed by reflective glass panes and juts out some 130 ft at both ends, supported by three large steel pillars. At the lower part of the building, occupying the same space as the roof, a vast podium gives access to the theatre and is, at the same time, a vantage point for the mural. The rest of the building is hidden behind a 50 ft. high structure of metal and glass panels, which serves as an anteroom to the complex. On the left are the elevator and access stairs, and on the right, the ticket offices. Inside, the backstage, the theater machinery and, in short, the entire complex, is contained in a stone structure.

Its location is known as the Zona Plateada, which explains the choice of silver and black for the framework of the theater-auditorium. The name refers to a now-defunct silver mine in the zone.

However, this color scheme is in contrast to the interior, where the bright reds and browns of the stage and adjacent areas, predominate. Once again, the architects wanted to give a classic feel to the building, recalling the great theaters of the past. The theater holds 2,000 and the installations include the latest in sound technology. Various studies were conducted to find the right definition of angles and distances to the stage. The center aisles were done away with so that people could move around between the rows and on the edges. This resulted in the acoustics being perfect at any point in the auditorium. Similarly, the insulating material lining the interior walls keeps out outside noise.

The building was completed in just eleven months, using material such as reinforced concrete, pre-cast concrete, steel, metal structures, and so on. Six concrete walls, each 2 ft. thick, were built in the center of the building, and another two outside support the entire roof. Some 1500 tons of steel were used, as well as 130 ft.-long frames and pre-cast concrete for the columns, beams, and paving. The lighting design was based on two concepts: serviceability and harmony with the architecture. To light the areas, small spotlights with indirect light were installed; they were brighter than usual because the building is also a concert hall.

Serviceability and aesthetics are perfectly integrated into this piece of architecture. The facade, finished in silver and dark gray, measures more than 43,000 sq. ft., and is made of a mixture of black granite, cement, and concrete aggregate, which together give the appearance of natural stone. The main materials used were 1,500 tons of steel, glass, metals, and pre-cast concrete.

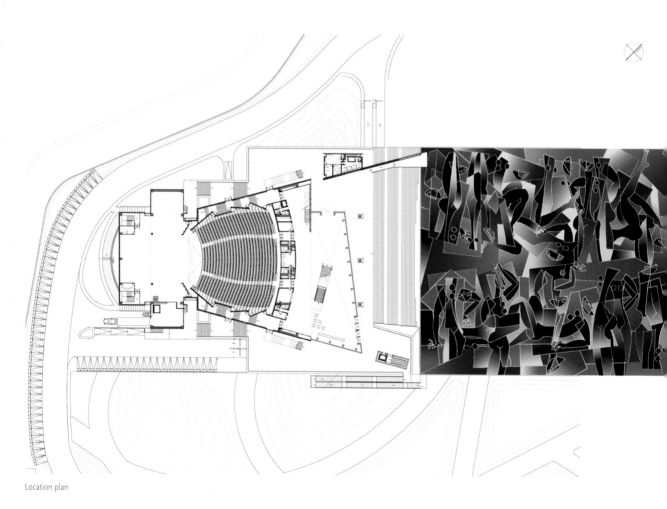

Location plan

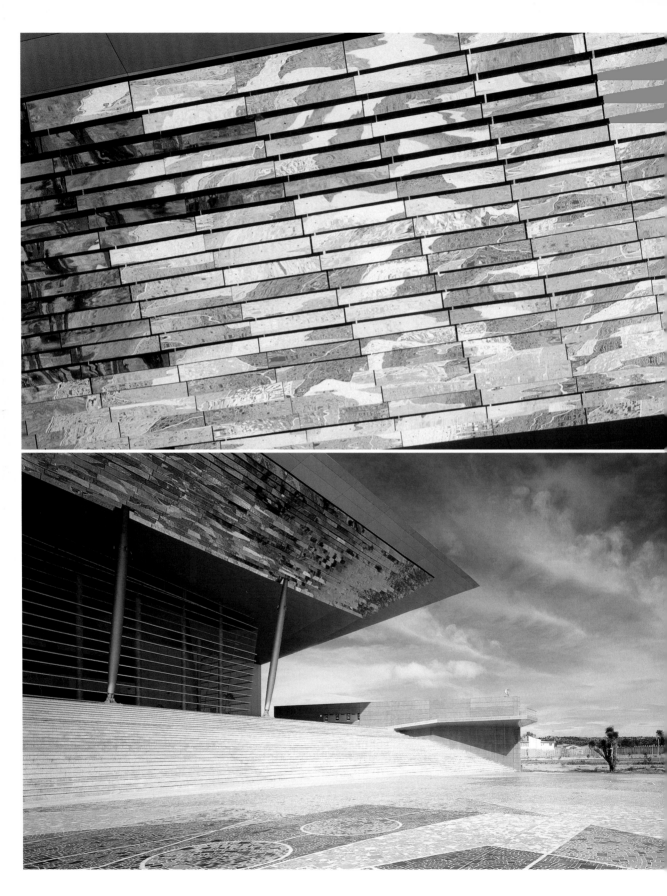

The architects decided to create a dialogue between the building and the immense 1,300-by-260 ft. mosaic situated in the central plaza of the David Ben Gurion Culture and Recreation Complex. The geometric shapes of Byron Gálvez's work are visually deconstructed in the reflecting glass panels 80 ft. from the ground. The primary colors contrast with the opaque gray shades that make up the facade of the theater-auditorium. The vestibule is framed by a glass and metal structure that lets in plenty of natural light, creating straight visual lines.

Photo © Emil Bos

Multiplex Cinecity-Limena

Limena, Italy   2005

ARCHITECT
Andrea Viviani/Viviani Architetti

CLIENT
Furlan Cinema e Teatri

PARTNERS
Marco Roboni (general supervisor); Martina Benetti, Alessandro Corrò, Andrea Manganaro, Giulia Tagliapietra; In.Pro (structure); Fiel (electricity); Studio Vescovi (plumbing and heating); Flaviano Favero (safety); CPM, Vitadello Intercantieri Spa (contractors); Arredamenti Moretti & Sons (fittings); Coges (metal); VenetaPav, Dorpetti (designs); Cogeme (special plastering)

AREA
99,028 sq. ft.

COST
25 million euros

PROGRAM
Large cinema complex (14 screens) with restaurants and children's play areas

Multiplex Cinecity-Limena is in Padua, a well-known Italian city with more than 3,000 years of history. It was one of the most important centers in the Roman Empire, and today is one of the richest Italian cities in art, with substantial civil and religious buildings and a large medieval wall. Padua is one of Italy's oldest, yet most dynamic cities, and over the years it has been forced to evolve and adapt to new trends in order to survive. There is a need to create new spaces to unite traditional buildings with new designs and businesses in step with the times we live in. Thus, Padua has become a cultural, yet commercial city that is visited by thousands of tourists all year long.

These were the circumstances that saw the birth of the cinema complex designed by Andrea Viviani, who had previously designed two projects with the same characteristics: the Cinecity Trieste and the Cinecity 2 Udine, in the cities of Trieste and Pradamano, respectively.

This cinema complex was built on an industrial estate in Limena, a small town of just 7,000 inhabitants 4 miles from Padua, that constitutes one of the economic centers of the Veneto region. Because the complex occupied a space that had previously been a factory, it needed to have an image that was entirely different from that of the surrounding buildings, to attract potential customers' attention. This has been achieved through the combination of materials, colors, and textures.

The fundamental core of the construction is stone, an element that withstands the passing of time very well. Subsequently, this stone core was clad in sections to draw attention to the building. The structure incorporates small aluminum panels that can regularly carry advertising, large opaque windows that let in natural light to the complex as well as small low-cost features, such as the floors that counteract the coldness of the stone and lend a warmer air to the structure while uniting it with the surroundings. It thus manages to combine the artificial elements it has with those provided by nature. The interior of the complex comprises 14 screening rooms, on two floors, with a total of 3,180 seats as well as a couple of restaurants and a children's play area. As with the exterior, the important thing in designing

the interior has been to obtain a unique, distinctive look with nothing to remind people of the industrial zone in which it is built.

The entrance is imposing as multiple features come into play. The architect decided to keep the existing features of the former factory but he painted them with vivid colors—such as red, black, green, and yellow—so that the customers do not relate them with the place's industrial past. The giant chessboard on the ceiling is one example. On entering, two small bathrooms greet the customers, who may take a while to realize what they are (the decoration combines plastic with aluminum and many colors). The colors in fact take on a significant role because the architect has opted for vivid, garish colors that grab the customers' attention and clearly mark a separation between the establishment and the different world of the exterior.

The idea is to create a space devoted to entertainment where people can forget their daily cares, and this begins with the first step taken in this cinema complex.

Color plays a leading role here. The best way to recreate a warm but attractive atmosphere is through hues that make an immediate impact. Colors such as red, black and green give a great deal of strength and vitality to the spaces. This sensation of warmth is also achieved with small accents of wood and the combination of the artificial lights.

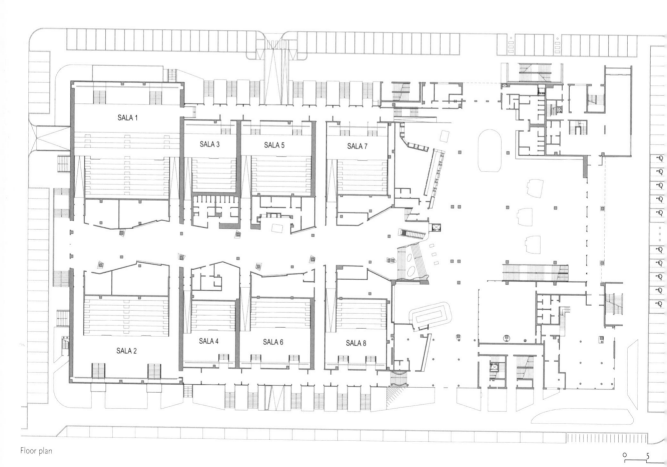

Floor plan

0   5

Even the smallest detail has been taken care of. For example, in one area
of the lateral facade, up to three different materials have been combined:
the stone of the main structure, plastic panels in a combination of colors,
and the aluminum used for the stairs that lead from the screening
rooms to the outside.

Photo © Dirk Wilhe

Gottlieb-Daimler Stadium

Stuttgart, Germany   2006

ARCHITECT
*ASP – Architekten Arat-Siegel & Partner,
Schlaich Bergermann & Partner, Weidleplan
Consulting*

CLIENT
Stuttgart City Council

SURFACE AREA
678,126 sq. ft.

COST
*First phase: 43 million euros
Second phase: 48 million euros
Third phase: 46 million euros*

PROGRAM
*Stadium for sports events such as football,
athletics, bicycle and motorcycle racing, boxing,
and concerts. Parking, shops, restaurant, VIP
lounge, pressroom*

Since 1993 the old Neckar Sports Stadium has been known as the Gottlieb-Daimler Stadium in honor of the German engineer and inventor. It dates back to 1933, when it was built to celebrate the Deutsches Turnfest German Athletics Meet). Historically, this stadium is a German icon because it is here that symbolic sporting events of great magnitude have been held. For instance, the first international match held in Germany after World War II was played here between the Swiss national side and the German team. On December 19th 1990, the same teams met again in the first international match to be played after German reunification. And, finally, it was one of the cities that hosted the World Cup Championships in 1974 and 2006. It is currently home to one of the most famous clubs in the German Bundesliga, VfB Stuttgart.

The stadium forms part of the Cannstatter Waser Sports Complex in the capital of the federal state of Baden-Wurtemberg, and lies at the heart of the 136-acre NeckarPark Stuttgart. It also hosts athletics championships, bicycle and motor cycle races, boxing matches, and can be used as a venue for spectacular concerts.

The renovation of the old stadium was carried out in three construction phases: the first phase took place from 1990 to 1993, the second phase from 1997 to 2001, and the third phase from 2004 to 2006. The most striking feature of this stadium is the spectacular construction on the roof consisting of a bow truss, with steel cabling and a synthetic textile membrane protecting the spectators' seats. The cabled structure and the roof membrane drew their inspiration from the shape of carriage wheels, which is a fixing structure that follows the principle of a horizontal center with a radial system of spokes. The membrane is constructed from 365,973 sq. ft. of PVC polyester fibers and is supported by a tower that ranges from 59 ft. at its base to 114.8 ft. at the top. These polyester fibers, together with a layer of fluorite, are 8 percent translucent, which means they allow a certain amount of sunlight to pass through. Some 2,700 tons of steel and 420 tons of steel cable were used to construct the roof structure, with its lattice design reminiscent of the vineyards in the vicinity of the sports complex. This original roof structure was built during the first phase,

along with other developments, such as the conversion of the stands into physical seats, new lighting, the installation of an electronic PA system, etc. Access points were also added for the disabled. The second phase included the renovation of the press area, the VIP enclosure, the office block, the parking lot and remodeling the grandstand, from one continuous bench into individual seats. To enable the stadium to be in conditions to host some of the World Cup matches in 2006, the third construction phase entailed major works of modernization, including improvements in the stadium entrance infrastructure, advancements in floodlighting, updating the sound system, and installation of huge video screens. The capacity of the stadium increased from the first construction phase to accommodate up to 55,896 spectators by the third phase. With respect to lighting, the most important technological advances were incorporated and designed in such a way that, if a total blackout were to occur, 1000 lx would be available. Two gigantic new screens were installed, with a total surface area of 2,475.7 sq. ft., making it the largest video system in Europe. Each screen measures 56.4 ft. by 23.7 ft. by 3 ft. and is capable of reproducing a 16:9 or 4:3 format, as required, with 603,136 pixels per screen. The sound system was improved to such an extent that it is now digitally controlled, with a maximum level of 120 decibels. So that the sound can be distributed perfectly, several experts worked over two days to adjust the system using special software programs. Another improvement in the infrastructure concerns the heating, which is regulated in keeping with outdoor temperatures and distributed by means of a network made up of more than 12.4 miles of piping buried 7.9 inches below the grass. Finally, the Business Center, which was the last section to be opened, was created. It has a large number of rooms of varying sizes ranging from 247.6 sq. ft. to 473.6 sq. ft. These can be hired every day of the week and are ideal places for conferences, meetings, courses and other events. A glass walkway provides access to the parking lot with more than 1,500 parking spaces.

The Stuttgart stadium stands out from other stadiums around the world on account of the spectacular forms of its striking roof. A roof structure made of steel cabling and a synthetic textile membrane fixed in position by means of a carriage-wheel system: a horizontal center with radial spokes. The roof rests on an outer frame supported by huge pillars ranging from 59 ft. to 114.8 ft. in height.

Modern developments and technological innovations required to host an important sports event were implemented during the third construction phase of the sports complex. At that time, new entrances for the general public were added, as was the Business Center, consisting of a large number of spaces and rooms for events and meetings. The building materials used inside are steel, reinforced concrete, glass, and wood.

Photo © Matteo Pia

Grey Lounge

Orzinuovi, Italy   2004

ARCHITECT
Marco Guido Savorelli

CLIENT
Luigi Pizzi

PARTNERS
Gabrielle Baglio; Daniela Bernabei; Curiosità di Anna Prosperi; DSB Progetti; Edilnova Commerciale; Morix; Vittorio Radice (interior fittings); Vissionnaire

AREA
1,722 sq. ft.

VOLUME
16,951 cu. ft.

COST
200,000 euros

PROGRAM
Music bar and discotheque

Between the Alpine foothills and the plain of Padania is the beautiful Italian city of Brescia, where the lifestyle is particularly comfortable and where it is easy to set up an industrial or commercial activity. It experienced a development upsurge after World War II and positioned itself as one of Italy's thriving economies.

The area's economic growth heralded the appearance of many new businesses and gave birth to this project. The owner is Luigi Pizzi, one of the most famous agents in the field of Italian art. His idea was to create a new establishment devoted to leisure that would be quite different than others in the city. He was looking for something more luxurious, more elegant, for people with greater spending power.

The importance of this building lies in its interior, which is why what normally draws the attention at the outset, the facade, plays a secondary role. This preference was due to the fact that the premises were designed to target a certain type of clientele. The space is divided into three clearly distinct zones: the bar area, the drinking area, and the dancing zone. It might seem that talk of

three zones refers to distinct elements that have nothing to do with each other, but this is not so. The three zones, all on the same level, become one through the materials and colors that are used, which provide the whole with a perfectly defined environment. Both the walls and ceiling are painted white, a color that lends elegance and also suggests that the premises are clean and spotless. The intention is to create a sensation of calm, a sensation that no other color would convey. The contrast and touch of modernity are achieved with small dark gray panels of varying sizes on different areas of the wall, giving rise to the creation of a classic space with a contemporary touch. The floor is covered in dark marble, which brings out the contrast with the predominantly white color of the walls and ceiling. This type of material has been used because it provides a natural look, is long-lasting, and is very easy to clean, features that need to be borne in mind when running an establishment for the public.

When selecting materials, the criterion was the search for contrast, and this is also noticeable in the decoration. The three

zones follow the same decorative underpinning: simple lines that avoid fussiness and anything that might be unattractive to potential customers, such as flashy decorative fittings that are completely unnecessary. The architect has opted for a minimalist decor, in other words a simple decor that does not neglect even the smallest details. The motto is "less is more," and the important thing is to link serviceability and design with the accessories that really are necessary.

This is why consistency has been the watchword in the use of colors and materials. This is because contrast must not only be echoed in the walls, floor, and ceiling of the establishment. The choice of fittings also plays a vital role, and here they are white, the tables are a gray aluminum color, and the bar is the same color as the panels installed on the walls.
The idea is to create an original and consistent space in order to establish a relaxed atmosphere for the customer.

The purity of the decorative lines and the color contrast are complemented with the use of artificial light. This has to be clear and direct, without producing shadows or leaving areas unlit. The best solution is halogen or downlights, as they meet this criterion to perfection, and they occupy less space than traditional light fittings.

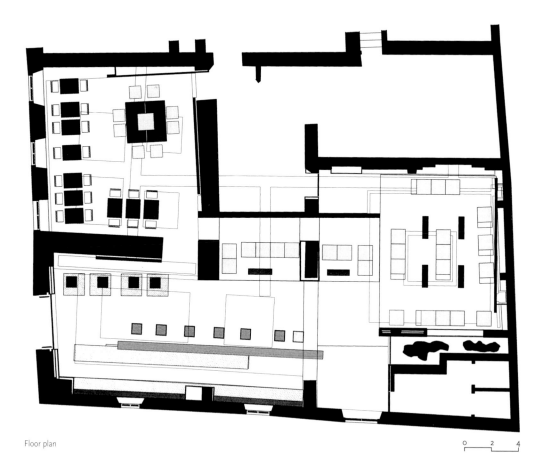

Floor plan

0   2   4

Photo © Yael Pinc

Universale Firenze

Florence, Italy   2000

ARCHITECT
Stefano Pirovano

CLIENT
Elettronolo, Tiziano Fagioli

PARTNERS
*RO.MA. (building contractor); Tecnoclima;
Zanussi; Gabellini Spa*

SURFACE AREA
15,435 sq. ft.

VOLUME
247,200 cu. ft.

COST
5 million euros

PROGRAM
Disco, restaurant, and bar

This former 1,000-seat movie theater has been converted into one of the most fashionable places in Florence. The building houses a restaurant, bar, and discotheque, and provides this Italian city with an exciting late-night venue. The theater was closed for more than 12 years and inevitably became a refuge for pigeons, which led to its deterioration. After three years of restoration and refurbishment, it once again saw the light of day and opened to the general public, thereby keeping the name and historic memory of the historic theater in the neighborhood of San Frediano. The Milan-based designer-architect commissioned to carry out the renovations drew up a project based on classical design and decoration. Likewise, the elegance and splendor of the history of the movies are reflected in the architecture inside the building. The new premises will pay tribute to its original use as a home for drama and movie stories, through the use of iconography and a wealth of references to the art form.

The building has several different areas: a stage for live concerts, three bars, a restaurant on the first floor and sufficient space to dance after-hours. The interior design and decoration are based on sheets of metal that have been cut by laser and soldered together, as is the case for the decorative elements on the main staircase, the banister and the mosaic on the floor. In the inner rooms, the aim was to reflect a certain sensuality that is associated with this type of architecture, which is displayed by means of rounded walls and oval structures that do not convey any idea of the rigidity commonly found with vertical and horizontal lines. The client and the architect both intended that these prerequisites should not involve too many risks that might lead to rapid aging. The whole building consists of three stories, which are interconnected by means of an escalator and an elevator. On the first floor is the lobby with a cloakroom to its right, leading directly to a bar. The discotheque is next door beside another small bar, which leads directly to the large concert hall. On the second floor is the restaurant, which has been refurbished as if it were an open-air patio even though it is really indoors. Also on this floor is a third bar. And finally, the restrooms are located in the basement.

The original cinema screens have been kept in their original place, and at night there are

continuous performances of the movies in video format. The films are classics of American movie history. For the live concerts, a roving TV camera has been set up to broadcast and screen images of the group that is on stage, along with pictures of the people who have come to see them.

The decoration hinges on the color gold, on the decorative stage, the chairs, and the dramatic stairway. The color is chosen to conjure up all the charm and glamour of the world of the silver screen. Other decorative elements include the colorful Cubist pictures of musical instruments, suggestive of musicals, and hearts, to pay tribute to romantic movies.

As far as the design's different shades of color are concerned, a warm palette has been chosen, typical of the evening hours when the building is open. The lighting is very theatrical, as dictated by the canons of the movie-making world, where flamboyancy would be counterproductive when intimacy and warmth are called for. So, yellowy hues and shades of red, brown, and black, which cast a faint light and create a silky-smooth atmosphere, are preferred. The main stairway, with its shades of gold, is majestic and dramatic. It has been designed to look like the stairs that Hollywood movie stars walk down in musicals from the golden age of the cinema.

The design and decoration of Universale revolve around the world of the silver screen, since the place was originally an old movie theater and playhouse. The range of colors chosen for this leisure palace are all warm with shades of gold, yellows, reds, browns, and blacks, which combine to give an elegant, albeit faint and tenuous light. The lighting has been designed not to be too strident, so as to convey the idea of intimacy and warmth required for this type of center.

Photo © Lluís R

5 Sentidos Lounge Bar

Empuriabrava, Spain   2006

ARCHITECT
Jordi Fernández, Eduardo Gutiérrez/
on_a arquitectura

CLIENT
Evaristo Gallego/Gallego World

PARTNERS
Xavier Badia (technical architect); Javier Escribano/Professional Assistent (installations engineer); Guillermo Beluzo, Marcelo Cortez (mock-up); Construccions Joan Fusté (builder); Laser Goded, Cmtpsl (metal); Cricursa, Vidres Gracia (glass); Aiterm (air conditioning); Talyali (painting); Quimipres (flooring); Fusteria Gironella (carpentry); Ramon Pujades (upholstery); Fredterm, Ergodec, Euromoble (fittings); CA2L (lighting); Joseph Ponsati (installation); Complas (acrylic glass); Retolam (vinyl); Pentamusic (acoustics)

AREA
2,315 sq. ft.

PROGRAM
Lounge bar

This bar is in a Mediterranean coastal town in Girona province. La Maria d'Empuriabrava is a large development built more than 30 years ago between Aiguamolls de l'Empordà and the bay of Roses, on land that was previously used for crops and grazing. The town stretches along a little more than 14 miles of navigable channels that form part of the Rivers Muga and Salins, and it is now the largest marina in Europe.

Because of its location, it can also be reached by air; its origin as a vacation home development means that it is packed during the summer. Most of these dwellings are similar in that they have a garden and boat access via the navigable channels that flow out to the sea. However, there are also areas with large apartment blocks as well as low-rise homes in which the permanent residents live.

The bar is situated in the area developed for the low-rise homes and occupies the bottom story of a two-story building. The client commissioned the architects to produce a project that met the following requirements: an original and exclusive design; a clear, but unique identity, a distinctive image; and above all, convenience for the customer.

The project occupies more than 2,315 sq. ft. of a previous business's premises: 1,500 sq. ft. are devoted to the bar, while the remaining area belongs to the patio. The architects' solution was the result of a conscientious analysis and a study of the former premises; furthermore, the interior space was planned according to the different types of customers using the bar. For example, the bar includes areas for groups, an area near the entrance for general use, an area for customers who are more used to this type of environment, and finally more private and flexible areas for other types of users. Although the interior is divided according to the preference of the customers, the structure is just one space that arouses a large number of perceptions in the user, in whom all the senses are exercised. This was why the owners decided to name the lounge bar "5 sentidos" (5 senses).

The architects drew their inspiration from the structure of a bone cell to produce the lay-out of the premises and distribution of the various spaces. These types of cell are characterized by the large number of adjoining cavities separated by a single material

that forms the walls and ceilings. The unique feature of these "walls" is that they are perforated; thus the material fulfils two functions at once: it divides the various spaces while maintaining a visual connection between them. The material chosen to bring about this twofold concept of division and connection was steel. With this material, the architects produced a three-dimensional web, with irregular shapes, deformed, stretched out, and consisting of 400 pieces of steel each 0.12 inch thick. A structure that is molded and adapted to the prior architectural scheme of the building covers the patio and also enables the creation of the interior spaces. The steel was laser-cut and folded to enable the multiple pieces to be connected in different ways, displaying more than 1,500 different faces. The large number of pieces, the connections, and the different layouts make each perspective unique and the light and reflections different at all times. The web was painted white to emphasize its presence over the black of the walls, ceilings, and floors. The ribbed sound-muffling on the walls and ceilings as well as the

typical fittings for a premises of this type were also painted black. For the flooring, black quartz with flecks of gray was chosen. The holes produced by the steel web are covered with large blue-tinged panes of glass in many different shapes.

The client wanted the lighting to change color depending on the suitability and time of year. To achieve this effect, the architects installed six separate banks of lights with an RGB fluorescent system so that any color can be obtained. This system also distinguishes between the interior zones.

The interior layout begins with a large swing door that opens onto an irregular-shaped rubber floorcovering and an extended magazine rack that turns into a long sofa covered in black fabric, surrounded by poufs covered in the same material. Then comes the bar and, on either side, two private areas whose fittings blend in with the walls. Beyond the private areas are the rest of the spaces which, with their televisions, armchairs, sofas, and stainless steel tables, continue the color scheme of the establishment, designed to highlight the white of the web.

The lighting color scheme for the lounge bar in winter is warm colors, and in the summer, cold ones; at night, greens and oranges predominate. As well as the general lighting, there are movable spots on the tables and ultraviolet lights in the floor; the paint on some of the bar counters reacts to ultraviolet light. The fittings are also painted in line with the desire to provide the establishment with contrasting colors which, at the same time, emphasize the white of the web, the project's principal feature.

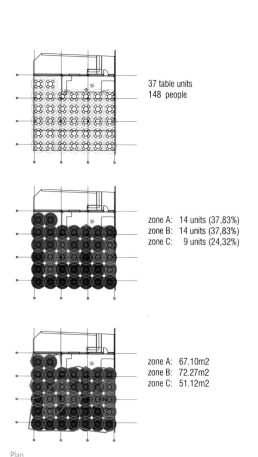

37 table units
148 people

zone A: 14 units (37,83%)
zone B: 14 units (37,83%)
zone C: 9 units (24,32%)

zone A: 67.10m2
zone B: 72.27m2
zone C: 51.12m2

Plan

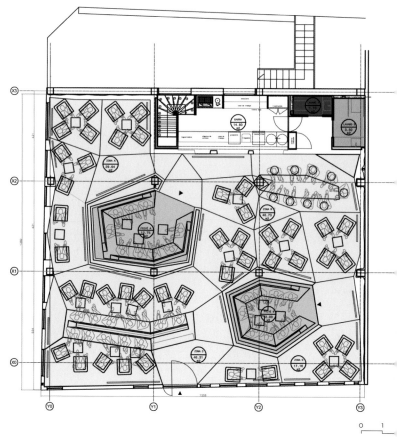

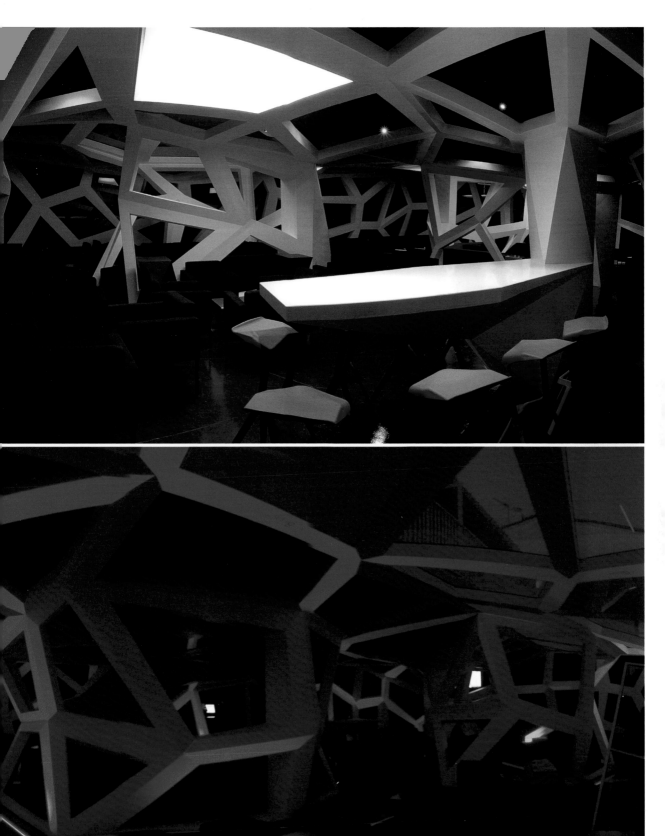

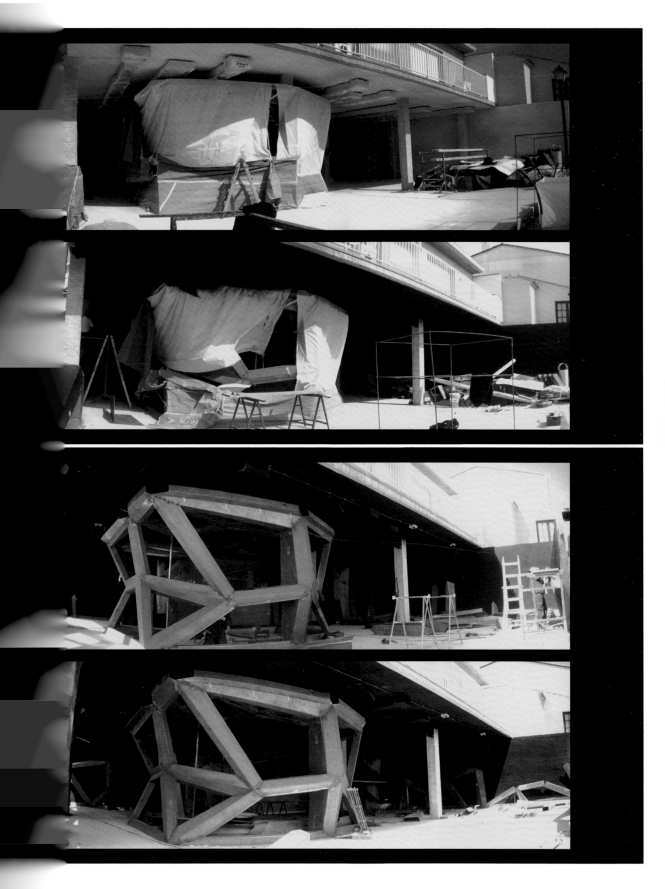

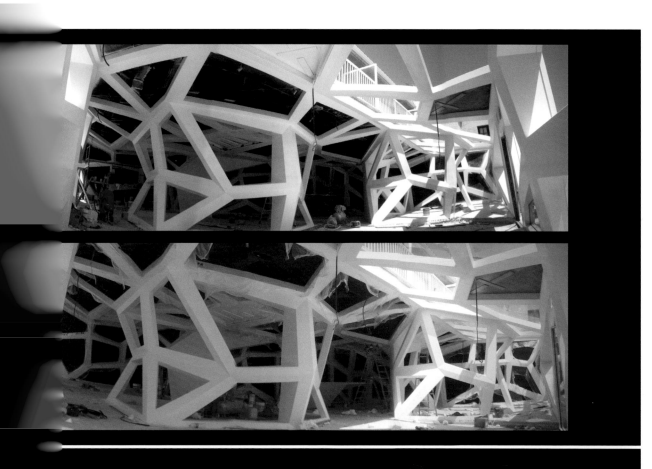

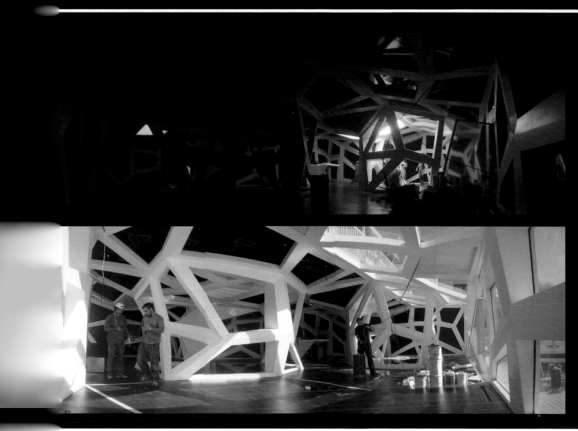

Photo © Roger Cas

Time Warner Center

New York, NY, U.S.A.   2004

ARCHITECT
SOM – Skidmore, Owings & Merrill

CLIENT
Columbus Centre, Related Companies, Apollo Real Estate Advisors

PARTNERS
WSP, Cantor Senuik Group, Philip Aviv & Associates (structure); Jenkins & Huntington (MEP engineering); Langan Engineering & Environmental Services (geotechnical engineering); Ken Smith Landscape Architect, Mathews Nielsen (landscape architect); Jerome S. Gilman Associates (consultant)

SURFACE AREA
2.8 million sq. ft.

COST
1,356 million euros

PROGRAM
Head office of Time Warner World, shops at Columbus Circle, Central Park, residence at the Mandarin Oriental Hotel, Jazz at the Lincoln Center, offices and parking facilities

The imposing, majestic architectural complex is located at Columbus Circle, on the southwest corner of Central Park, in Midtown Manhattan. The site is composed of two glass towers, soaring to a height of 755 ft., with 80 stories apiece, which were designed to house the main offices of the AOL Time Center. In this project, not only have the two skyscrapers been erected, but one of the most ambitious urban development projects of the first decade of the century has been put together around them: namely, the project called One Central Park. This complex has now become the cathedral and symbol of the digital age.

This architectural site is composed of the Mandarin Hotel, the new 5-star hotel with luxury accommodation for 251 guests, facilities for meetings, banquets, and other public areas. There are also condominiums or residential tenement blocks. Time Warner World, Inc. has occupied an entire third of the building as office space on the lower floors of the complex. There are also other offices, which have been taken up by their associate companies and a TV studio for CNN. On the ground floor is the shopping

mall at Columbus Circle, consisting of luxury stores, restaurants, and a public area for entertaining visitors to the Center. Jazz at Lincoln Center is the first and only performance space in the world created specifically for jazz musicians. Their facilities include 3 venues, a recording studio, and classrooms. To complete the list of spaces that form part of the architectural site, a subway station was also built here, along with parking facilities on three different levels to accommodate 540 vehicles. Apart from the complicated infrastructure typical of such huge complexes, such as access points, facilities and the underground car parks, it also includes all the latest advances in technology. There are complete wireless coverage and broadband facilities throughout the entire building. Culture, entertainment, technology, and sophistication all come together inside these twin towers.

Because of the enormous size of the building and its complex program, the site exemplifies the concept of a city within a building as opposed to the more usual situation of a building inserted in a city. The shapes and design of the buildings adapt to the urban

context to which they belong: the network of Manhattan. For example, the previously eliminated 59th Street has been restored again. This is a public east-west artery, which is particularly important because it also serves as the southern boundary of Central Park. This corridor is re-created by building a huge transparent space which is open to the general public. This space measures the same width as the street, which penetrates the building in a westerly direction until it reaches the very heart of the project. The civic functions usually performed in the street are located in this case inside the building, such as the shops. Furthermore, it is possible to enjoy watching the cultural, public activity of the Jazz at Lincoln Center right from the heart of the Center itself. Another example of the Time Warner Center's adaptation to the urban context in which it is located is the curvature of the front of the building, in keeping with Columbus Circle, which reinforces the previously eroded form of this urban element, which is one of its kind in neo-baroque style. Finally, the urban network comes to an end along the north-south axis of the towers, distorted from the octagonal grid of the city, into the shape of a parallelogram. Visually, the axis is aligned exactly on the skyline with the angle of Broadway, divided into two by Columbus Circle. And therefore it seems as though 59th Street passes right through the architectural complex in the space between the two towers.

As is often the case in buildings of this nature in the Big Apple, the most important building materials are glass and steel, which are most apparent on the front of the building. This type of facade functions as a real mirror reflecting the urban landscape of New York. The rectangular patterns on the glass curtain facade reflect the Manhattan street grid. In order to increase the safety of the building, it was decided to use concrete for the pillars, stairways, and fire escapes (very common in buildings in Europe).

On the ground floor of the Time Warner Center is Columbus Circle, with its luxury stores, restaurants, and public area. These civic functions are typical of a street outdoors, but in this case they are located inside the building, as though they formed part of a shopping mall. This is due to the intent of the architects and clients to construct a large transparent space open to the general public, which links the main artery 59th Street to the heart of the project.

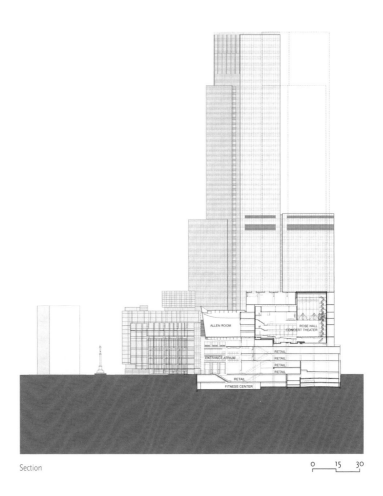

Section

0   15   30

Photo © Richard Dav

Selfridges Birmingham

Birmingham, U.K.   2003

ARCHITECT
Future Systems

CLIENT
Selfridges & Co

PARTNERS
Arup (general contractors);
Boyden & Co (topography)

SURFACE AREA
269,100 sq. ft.

COST
91 million euros

PROGRAM
Shopping and leisure center, shops,
restaurants, bars

Both the clients and the architects wanted to create a building that would provide the English city of Birmingham with a modern architectural icon. They situated it in the area of the Bull Ring, next to a neo-gothic church of the 19th century, so that it would function as a catalyst to breath new life into the district of Digbeth. The visual contrast between this new building and the church was done on purpose and serves to attract the attention of city visitors and inhabitants alike. In spite of this contrast in shapes, materials, modes and colors between the ancient buildings adjacent to the new one, they coexist in perfect harmony. Such harmony is achieved by means of the soft textures of curved shapes integrated in the urban landscape and inspired by nature.

The client, Selfridges, was aware of the crisis that the buildings of large department stores go through in favor of suburban shopping centers. That is why they commissioned the English architects to design a building that would reinterpret the role of this type of business within the city itself. A building was erected for such purposes with a design that has great visual impact and

uses its architecture like an advertisement. The structure is completely curved in all directions, and therefore there is no distinction between the walls and ceilings. Neither are there any right angles that interrupt the flowing, continuous lines based on organic shapes. For example, the external appearance of this biomorphic structure looks like the skin of a snake covered in scales or the structure of numerous panels in a fly's eye. The design of the front of the building is striking because of its impermeable layer of 15,000 shiny, aluminum discs, bereft of all color, resting on a concrete surface, painted an intense blue—the blue invented by Yves Klein. This then is a clear example of architecture treated as a sculptural work of art. The sunlight reflected on the front of the building varies according to the atmospheric conditions and the number of hours of daylight, acquiring different and constantly changing colors and visual textures.

This desire for a spectacular, dramatic effect has been transferred to the interior, where each floor has been conceived by different designers such as Stanton Williams, Aldo Cibic and Eldridge & Smerin. The interior is

composed of a spectacular atrium which receives the direct rays of the sun through an enormous skylight in the roof of the building. The artificial light is adapted to this entry of natural sunlight, determining the spectacular nature of the internal landscape, with the interplay of snatches of light, shadows and reflections. The escalators meet around the atrium with an eye-catching curved design. The original distribution and color chosen—bright white—gives it a plastic appearance. The stair lining consists of sculptural elements made of reinforced plastic with fiberglass fixed to the steel frame. In order to achieve this type of continuous surface, the joints were sealed with a fabric made of fiberglass and synthetic resin. There are large openings in the sides of the wall, following the sinuous design that is a feature of the shopping center. These openings are windows, which make it possible to see in and out. In spite of the modern method of execution that is noticeable in the design, the architects did not refrain from using traditional architectural resources that are commonly found in large department stores, such as atriums, skylights, escalators and forecourts. Access to the warehouses can be via four entrances: the main entrance to the shopping center; the one leading to the cladding on the patio, above St Martin's Church; from the corner of Moor Street and Parl Street; and finally, from the bridge leading to the parking lot. Therefore, the intention of representing the fluid form of the outside of the building is likewise achieved in the interior of the building, by means of this organic atrium which organizes and arranges the layout of the store.

Although the vast building should be perceived as a solid, robust shape on the skyline of the city, its external appearance seems absolutely weightless, akin to a live body that is just about to move. This extraordinary, innovative project has set a new milestone in architectural constructions for shopping centers.

This spectacular plasticity displayed by the facade of the building, treated as though it were an architectural sculpture, is also reflected in the interior of the building. The various different levels are distributed around an enormous atrium, with shops, a luxury restaurant, a patio, etc. The atrium is completely lit up by a glass skylight in the roof, which allows the natural sunlight to penetrate in dramatic fashion, creating the interplay of light and shade inside. The immaculate whiteness of the escalators is the main focus of the design, affording it the elegance demanded by the clients for a large department store.

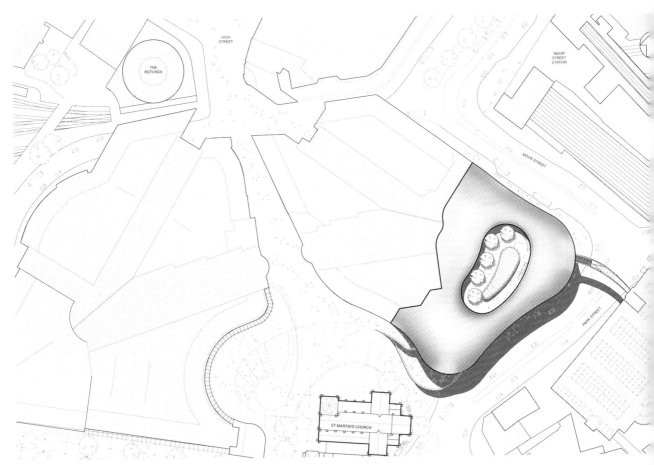

Location plan

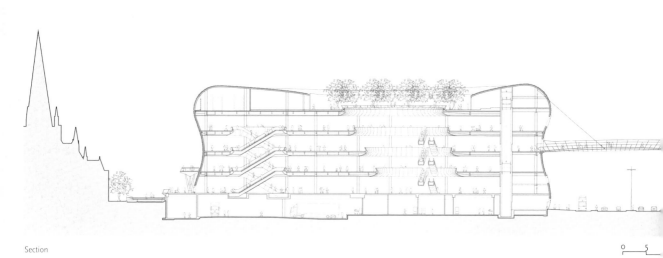

Section

Photo © Benny Ch

Costume National

Los Angeles, CA, U.S.A.   2000

ARCHITECT
Marmol Radziner & Associates

CLIENT
Costume National Clothing Corporation

PARTNERS
*Marmol Radziner & Associates, Ross Yeridan,
Reginald Dunham (building contractor);
Marmol Radziner & Associates (landscape
architecture); Niver Enignnering (structural
engineering); John Brubaker (lighting); Marmol
Radziner & Associates (interior designer); Ardex
(floor); Geisler's Glass (glass); Monte Allen
(decoration); Bartco (LED engineering)*

SURFACE AREA
2,600 sq. ft.

PROGRAM
Building that houses a clothing boutique

Situated in Melrose Avenue, in the West Hollywood section of Los Angeles is the new store of the Italian firm, Costume National. The architects reconverted an old building that had housed a restaurant and gave it a new look inside and out. The building occupies approximately 2,600 sq. ft. right in the heart of the buoyant Melrose commercial district, which includes other well-known firms such as Miu Miu, Liza Bruce, and Fred Segal.

The design is undeniably minimalist in its concept of space and elegant all at the same time, which is typical of a clothes boutique selling haute couture.

The intention of the clients is that the new boutique should provide a strong visual identity, which should reflect the spirit of Los Angeles along with the conceptual philosophy of a brand name like Costume National. Therefore, the challenge of the architects was to resolve this need for visual impact in a spatial context that is typical of a shop with these characteristics. The outcome was a plan that was painstakingly designed so as to reflect the philosophy of the firm in a natural way. Therefore, the

architects obtained a dynamic atmosphere through the use of split level in the interior, emphasized by the zenithal lights that illuminate the whole space from the ceiling right down to the floor. This split-level design also affords a sensation of weightlessness accentuated by the range of whites employed and by the indirect light distributed by various lamps. These lamps are hidden behind the structures supporting the clothes hangers.

The dynamic nature of the space is also materialized in the two main facades of the building: both glazed, with large windows that allow you to see into the inside of the shop from the street. They function as a shop window displaying the wares sold inside. The use of large windows is also due to the desire to maximize the height of the place and take advantage of the natural light. In spite of the innovations, the building still follows the same line as shops where this textile brand is distributed all over the world, although the result gives the establishment an atmosphere that is typical of Los Angeles, through its fresh interpretation of the city's culture. It draws inspiration from

CoSTUME NATIONAL

the dress-making techniques and textile construction of the firm, Costume National.

The special distribution on different levels inside the shop plays with the dimensions of the human figure. In some parts the level of the ceiling is much closer to the visitor and in others it is sloping, so that the distance is much further from the floor. Inside the shop there is plenty of space to sit down, as if it were a sanctuary, and there is a private section that functions like a changing room. The construction of shelves running around the walls from floor to ceiling, sometimes reaching a height of nearly 9 ft., pay tribute to the minimalist sculptor, Donald Judd. As for the decoration, the feeling of luxury in the place is achieved by means of the studied variety of textures, colors, and fabrics, such as the chairs in various shades of brown leather and suede upholstery. The veneered wood finish in shades of gray, the white stainless steel panels and the glass with its bias lighting thanks to fiber optics are more elements of the original scheme of décor.

With this composition of different materials, the designers have tried to achieve a counterpoint that is ideal for the modern-day aesthetics of Costume National. The final outcome is an environment that is perfect for housing the fashion items of the Italian firm.

Elegance and minimalist design are the parameters chosen to set off the line in textiles marketed by the high-fashion boutique from Milan. Both the furniture and also the display panels and shelves inside are specially made following a style that is typical of Los Angeles. In addition, the same line is taken as in all the other boutiques belonging to the Italian firm all over the world. A simple range of color is used for decoration, such as the whites for the panels, pearl gray for the floor, browns in leather, and suede for the furniture and pale yellows, which add depth to the surrounding environment.

Photo © Joan Mune

ArtQuitect

Barcelona, Spain   2000

ARCHITECT
José Luis López Ibáñez/Inmat Arquitectura

CLIENT
ArtQuitect

SURFACE AREA
2,150 sq. ft.

PROGRAM
Showroom for bathroom fittings

The aim of the firm ArtQuitect was to announce the start of a new era, using a new context to display the special features of their star product, the bathroom. In order to do this, they hired the Murcia-based architectural studio, which drew up a project based on two objectives. The first of these was to create a showcase that would combine the client's ideas while providing a setting for all the novelties, ranges, stands, Vola accessories, washbasins, Rapsel accessories, and Bardelli and Academia surfaces and linings. The second objective was to bring together in the same context the latest innovations in ceramic washbasins in order to define the specialty of the company that markets all the aforementioned products.

This new contribution to the world of commercial showcases was to be developed on premises located in a historical neighborhood in the old part of Barcelona. The new premises would be located on the ground floor of a building dating back to the beginning of the last century, whose structure has unusual building features. The internal layout of the area is arranged over two very different sections. The first section is at the

front of the building and has a rectangular floor plan, with three glass cavities. The central cavity provides access to the showcase area. The architectural work in this area consisted of lining the space with cardboard and plaster, eliminating past irregularities and organizing the area in straight lines, so as to create a sort of white box with continuous surfaces. Two longitudinal fluted channels were made in the false ceiling in order to install the background lighting, which would emphasize the spirit of the firm's main theme. The lighting is diffused over the showcases to avoid any unnecessary interplay of light and shadow. The second section has a rectangular floor plan, fragmented by a central area composed of a small-scale compartment and two superimposed staircases leading respectively to the basement and offices, on a higher level.

Once the site had been examined, the architects studied how to reflect the client's requirements. For this purpose, they looked to the concept of dreams as the beginning of each new creative process. They took as their starting point the fact that, before coming into being, all objects first appear in the

designer or creator's imagination, and are then materialized, becoming tangible and real. In keeping with this premise, the principal idea the architect wished to reflect in the showcase emerged: Without dreams, matter can never become an object. This principle was expressed as a reality through the creation of graphics of Fornasetti's enigmatic female faces, applied to poetic situations. Thus, a journey is created through the various areas of the set design, where the products on display become the main components of a series of imaginary moments.

In the first area, a black face with white vinyl is constructed to dramatize the initial idea: contrasted primary elements, black and white. This is followed by a single, horizontal, linear corridor running the length of a translucent plane with no variations in its path since it is designed as a theme that flows in one direction. The translucent plane is constructed from a lightweight portable structure with galvanized steel sections. Sheets of translucent polyester are riveted to

the structure to form a kind of membrane. This arrangement is not unintentional, since the idea is to achieve a transparency that expresses ambiguity, and with this purpose in mind, the membrane should have a thickness of 0.08 in. In addition, the Fornasetti faces are printed on square, 3.9 by 3.9 ft. windows that form part of the structure. These figures are displayed in various symbolic forms: circular watches, light-bulbs, waning moons, candies, goblets, and star shapes. They are the dreams depicted in the history of art by masters of Surrealism. These windows with their revolving structure set up the meeting between the visitor and the product. The light in this area transforms completely to provide a constant, zenithal and magical illumination that contrasts with the shop section. In order to achieve this effect, spotlights are placed directly above the steel cables, enhancing their color.

The resulting atmosphere of such a laborious design is culminated with the repetition of sounds to recreate a dreamlike mood.

At the end of the section there are four modules measuring 4.3 by 4.3 by 9.8 ft., which run from the floor up to the false ceiling. These structures are made of varnished steel and are covered with polyester so as not to clash with the other elements, which act as individual display cubicles exhibiting the new washbasins. Reflective glass plates are fitted to the inside creating spatial multiplicity and the interplay of shape and form.

el guiño la despedida, ¿por qué n
el sueño llega a su fin, y el obj
en forma de luz

Photo © Paul Tahon & Ronan Bourou128

Tiles in the Kvadrat Showroom

Stockholm, Sweden   2006

ARCHITECT
Ronan & Erwan Bouroullec

CLIENT
Kvadrat AS

PARTNERS
Dinesen Floors (flooring); A-Z Snedkeriet, Esbjerg (fittings); Sweco Interior Architects (architects); Claus Mølgaad (textile engineering); Fagerdala Cellplaster (manufacturers), Vincent Muracciole (lighting consultant)

AREA
2,690 sq. ft.

PROGRAM
New Kvadrat Showroom with tiles system

In the final years of the 20th century and the beginning of the 21st century, consumerism has become a leisure-focused activity. The rise of the consumer culture has brought about more widespread competition in the commercial sector. Stores display increasingly more striking and intelligent designs, aimed at attracting the consumer who finds himself saturated with a vast choice of products. This means that the role of designers is one of the most important in the process of winning new customers. They create designs based on the serviceability of the product but with touches of seduction and imagination in order to heighten desire for the item on display. They design showrooms that are more imaginative, more dramatic, with spectacular ideas, using materials that attract the attention of shoppers.

In this case, the client commissioned a team of architects specializing in the permanent research and development of technical solutions for artistic purposes to design a scenario for the launching of a new line of textile samples in Stockholm. The textile company, Kvadrat, is famous for developing and supplying high-quality material with an experimental design, the starting point for the most innovative creations on the market. The firm's usual collections consist of curtain fabrics, wall hangings, fabric screens that separate spaces and furniture. Artists and designers work together to create these designs with the most up-to-date technology, giving free rein to experimentation.

The architects specifically designed what is known as the tiles system, a system that consists of the laying out of independent textile structures with acoustic isolation, to act as dividing screens. The pieces are folded and interlaced forming pleats by means of a weave that links them. This assembly enables the opening up or closing of openings depending on one's needs. The main objective is to specifically highlight the variety of textures and materials of the collection. This system provides a spatial decor that supplies sensuality and warmth to the whole. One of the most amazing features of this system made up of small pieces is the freedom to change the layout and atmosphere of the area. Thus, it gives the showroom a certain flexibility and a wide range of potential changes and modifications.

The walls are conceived of as independent and self-sufficient modules which, because they are formed by small mobile structures, can be quickly and easily moved. They are designed as true movable boxes, typified by their easy handling and distribution. The properties of this system mean that access, corridors and openings can be changed and thus a fully flexible space usage can be obtained.

This tiles system is also a new way of building the walls with independent modules, in the tradition of their well-known algues and twigs concept. It is the result of a great deal of thought, planning and development in the construction of soundproofed spaces using fabric. Whether they are organic or geometric pieces, the tiles can create infinite shapes within a scale system. Thus this sys-

tem, characterized by its great flexibility, provides multiple uses and applications for the layout of autonomous soundproofed spaces. The variety of color shades used in these spaces depends on the main product in the showroom. Thus the colors of the fabrics are represented in the textile walls: ranges of greens, blues, grays, yellows, and oranges.

The manufacture and creation of these tiles is a rapid, convenient, and easy process. The hard base made of foam is molded between two pieces of material at high speed and in a very short space of time. With this easy-to-use system, anyone can install variable and geometric surfaces. The result is the construction of walls and dividers with a soft, rhythmic appearance, giving rise to spectacular spaces in tranquil surroundings.

For the presentation of a Kvadrat showroom in Stockholm, the architects designed a system of textile structures with soundproofing. The tiles system, as it is known, is for soundproofing walls dividing different spaces, for independent fittings or as doors to independent spaces. These textile walls are formed by pieces that are folded and interlaced, thus forming pleats. This system is surprisingly easy to install.

To emphasize the variety of materials and textures of this textile firm, the designers used a broad range of colors. The different shades of green, blue, gray, yellow, and orange are represented on the textile walls and reflect the star products of the display. These structures can be removed, created afresh, can incorporate openings, or move at any time thanks to their simple assembly.

Photo © Matteo Piaz

Icebergs Bondi

Sydney, Australia   2002

ARCHITECT
Lazzarini Pickering Architetti

PARTNERS
Tanner Architects (executive architect);
Lazzarini Pickering Architetti (lighting);
Massimiliano Baldieri, Rick Cale, Geoff Thorne,
Phillip Hodge/Clipsal (lighting consultants);
Scott Wilson Irwin Johnston (consultants);
Easton Buiders NSW (contractor), MsW
Projects/Doug Coombes (project manager);
Van der Meer Bonser (engineering);
PKA Acoustic Consulting (acoustics);
Skye McCardle (coordination)

PROGRAM
Restaurant and lounge bar

The architects' main objective was to build an area that would be a restaurant, bar and dining room all in one. This establishment had to be converted into one of the most spectacular places in Sydney, and it had to reflect the intimate, friendly character sought by one of the largest restaurant owners in Australia, Maurice Terzini. The restaurant occupies the upper floor of the Icebergs Pavilion, located on the south side of Bondi Beach in the Australian city.

The original area was a long corridor, similar to a passageway, measuring 164 by 16.4 ft., which lent itself to a claustrophobic atmosphere. However, the architects decided to use a design that would opt for a spacious, open-plan, elegant, and sophisticated area. The restaurant owner, a fan of small, intimate spaces, decided that the atmosphere should be that of a beach house rather than the usual restaurant style. Therefore, small spaces were created that would guide the clients' attention towards the spectacular views of the famous Bondi shoreline.

The result was the creation of different areas such as a dining room, bar, small waiting area, reception, the kitchen, two groups of restrooms, and the terrace surrounding the establishment. On the western side is a luxury dining room seating 90 people distributed over different sections adjacent to the bar. On the east, the reception area, which leads to two more dining rooms: one for large groups and the other for more intimate gatherings. These areas are separated by glass panels suspended from the ceiling, to create a warm atmosphere and provide more comfortable dining facilities. The sensation of having more space is achieved by means of semicircular structures and mirrors arranged in strategic fashion.

The lighting required is natural light coming in through large windows situated at various points around the restaurant. These windows function as vantage points; they provide views of the sea and the Australian coastline. It was designed in this way because the client and the architects wanted to give more importance to the lighting and thus be able to create a cool, spacious area. At night the artificial light is controlled in such a way as to create different atmospheres for the various different spaces inside the restaurant. The spectacular natural

scenery during the day needs to find an equivalent when night falls. According to Terzini: "if the lighting is controlled, the atmosphere is controlled." The lighting project is based on four circular tube-shaped chandeliers in the ceiling, which are situated in most of the communicating areas around the restaurant: the entrance, reception, the waiting area, and the bar. Owing to the many surfaces of Icebergs, it was essential to exert control over the lighting. The original idea was to combine lighting with candles superimposed on top of the chandeliers, but this was rejected for safety reasons. Instead, an innovative system was used involving the use of small lamps designed as if they were candles, emitting a light with a similar strength. Every 20 seconds, the lighting is moved thanks to a system of electromagnetic pulses.

The acoustics have also been attended to in great detail. The two areas are different in terms of character and number of people and therefore have been refurbished carefully for different levels of sound. For the largest tables, and therefore the noisiest, the capacity to absorb the acoustic frequency has been intensified. For example, the music coming from the bar is not noticeable from the areas of more intimate conversation.

All the decoration revolves around achieving chromatic shades and textures that match the marine environment, so care is taken with even the slightest, most insignificant details. The fabrics used for the armchairs, cushions, and tablecloths, emulate the blues, turquoises, and aquamarines of the seawater on a sunny day. To represent a rainy day or a cloudy afternoon, greens and purples are used. One of the elements that stands out most in the interior decor are the chairs in the shape of a C hanging from the ceiling. These are mobile and allow conversation to take place while admiring the spectacular scenery.

In the Icebergs restaurant there is an area with rooms intended to accommodate only a few diners. These intimate spaces are separated from one another by glass panel structures suspended from the ceiling. In order to achieve greater visual amplitude, mirrors are placed in strategic positions to reflect the interior space. Large windows have been inserted to offer guests spectacular views of the sea and Sydney coastline, while enjoying the delicious fare of one of the best restaurants in Australia.

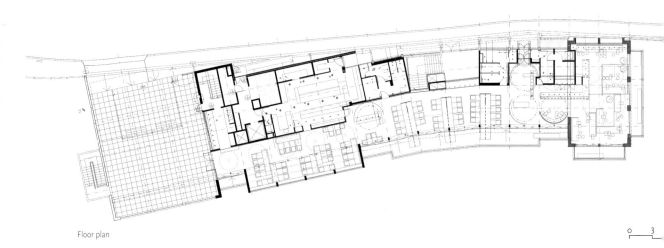

Floor plan

0   3

One of the most important sections on the premises is the bar, located right at the very center of the establishment. The lighting for the area is optimal thanks to the natural light that penetrates through the huge windows during the day and the artificial light provided by enormous chandeliers suspended from the ceiling. The interior decor is based on the color blue, since it was hoped to integrate the context of the sea outside with the textures featured in the interior design. The huge glass windows also function as doors leading to the terrace, where large glass panels act as a parapet providing protection from the wind.

Photo © Mark Ballogg, Rockwell Group

SushiSamba Rio

Chicago, IL, U.S.A. 2003

ARCHITECT
David Rockwell, David Mexico, Edmund Bakos, Marc DeSmet, Josh Held/Rockwell Group

CLIENT
Shimon Bokovza, Danielle Billera, Mathew Johnson

PARTNERS
Sara Duffy (interior designer); Metro Design Associates (MEP engineering); Culinary Design and Fixture (consultant); Focus Lighting (lighting); FTL Happold Design and Engineering (structure consultant)

PROGRAM
Restaurant, bar, cabaret

This restaurant is one of the four establishments the New York SushiSamba group owns in Miami, Tel Aviv, Chicago, and New York. The restaurant chain creates a remarkable fusion between three different cultures. The original result comes from a mixture of Brazilian, Japanese, and Peruvian cultures, which are echoed in the architecture, music, and cuisine. This cultural union originated at the beginning of the last century, when Japanese émigrés traveled to South America in search of fertile land to make their fortunes with coffee plantations. This happened above all in the capitals of Peru and Brazil. As time went by, these cultures gradually blended together and led to new concepts in various fields. In cuisine, ingredients such as miso soup and sushi combine with ceviche and beef, accompanied, for example, by Brazilian spirits. It is a perfect flavor combination between native Japanese cuisine and typical South American dishes.

One of the most striking aspects for the visitor is the facade, with a design that sets it apart from the adjoining buildings. The New York architects designed a facade with straight lines and typical Brazilian colors:

yellows, greens, lilacs, and so on. These lines are typical of Mondrian's abstract compositions, which contrast with the rest of the brick buildings on Chicago's North Wells Street. The doors have been designed following the style of the facade: primary-color transparent glass and handles created especially for the building.

The design also makes use of the festive colors of Brazil's carnival, together with zoomorphic figures that are typically Asian.

Once they go through the main door, diners find themselves in a roomy area where the main feature is an oval bar made of bamboo and illuminated terrazzo. Inside the bar are illuminated plaques and glass cases with shapes that look like pieces of ice. Over the bar hangs a type of curtain made of small pearls. These decorative features re-create the carnival atmosphere of Rio de Janeiro. This sparkling curtain can be found in all the areas and acts as a wall dividing two different settings from the floor to the ceiling, or as a decorative wall hanging from the ceiling. The bar is designed for those who wish to enjoy observing the oval structure where the dishes they are going to eat are put

together. Passing through, one comes to the main dining area, which surrounds the bar and goes through to the end of the restaurant. Here, there are intimate spaces for couples as well as more public spaces for large groups. The terrazzo floor of the main dining area has multicolor backlighting, which constantly moves in the manner of a samba dance. The ceiling lamps have volumetric structures that represent southeast Asian jellyfish. The furniture is of hardwood brought directly from Brazil; the seats are covered in leather or green and orange fabric, following the aesthetic line of the whole place. Alcoves have been placed on the south wall of the dining area for semiprivate parties for up to 10 guests, with views of the main dining area and the bar. Between the main dining area and a private room there is a circular area at a lower level, also for semi-

private parties. They are separated by silvery pearl curtains that drop from the ceiling to the floor. A subsequent private dining room with room for a hundred diners is designed for business functions that require a certain amount of privacy. The main feature is the color red: crimson fabrics, fiery glass, and lenticular panels on a floor in shades of brown. This area transports the visitor to underground Chicago.

Finally, a stairway that imitates a DJ booth leads to the garden dining area on the second floor. The decorative plants and the design evoke the peaceful atmosphere of Japan and at the same time, the fragrant air of Brazil. This terrace is closed in with glass panels during the winter and is opened up in summer to enable customers to dine in the open. This establishment has become one of Chicago's favorite fashionable haunts.

The private dining area at the south end of the restaurant was designed for private companies that are looking for a more intimate atmosphere. The design is reminiscent of underground Chicago, with classic red fabric-covered banquettes and wooden panels in various shades of brown on the floor. A lilac-colored pearl curtain hangs from the ceiling and separates the area before the main dining area.

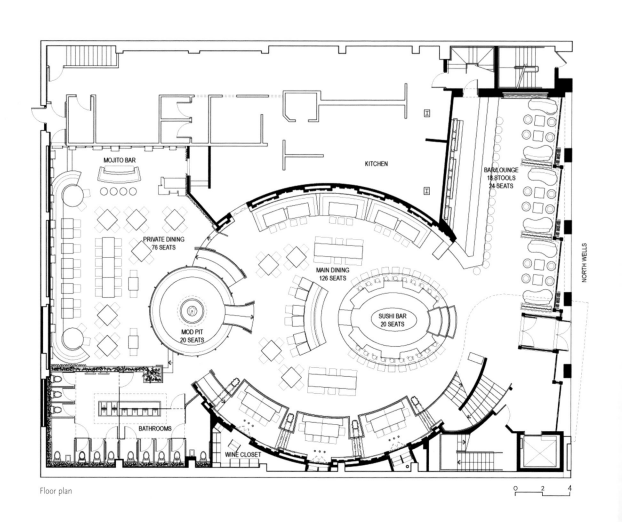

Floor plan

0 2 4

An oval central bar is the main feature of SushiSamba Rio's main dining area. The most common materials used for the interior are bamboo for the furniture and terrazzo for the floor. Illuminated glass cases in the bar look like pieces of crushed ice; jellyfish-shaped lamps light the ceiling. These elements are clear examples of the hybrid design—a mixture of Oriental and South American cultures, that is also the touchstone of the cuisine.

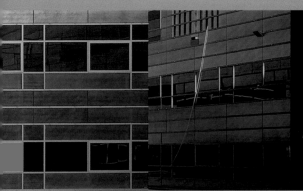

Public Buildings, Institutions & Offices

Public Services Buildings
Corporate Buildings
Convention & Exhibition Centers
Hybrid Centers
Training Centers
Skyscrapers

Photo © Rob't H

Rijkswaterstaat Zeeland Head Office

Middelburg, Netherlands   2004

ARCHITECT
Architectenbureau Paul de Ruiter

CLIENT
Rijksgebouwendienst (government building agency)

PARTNERS
ABT adviseurs in bouwtechiek, Velp (construction management and builder); Halmos (installations); moBius consult (construction work); Bosch Slabbers Tuin en Landschapsarchitecten (landscape architecture); Dan Peterman (artist); BVR adviseurs stedelijke ontwikkeling landschap en infrastructuur, Palmboom & van der Stedenbouwkundigen (urban development); BAM Utiliteitsbouw (general contractor)

SURFACE AREA
127,585 sq. ft.

VOLUME
1.43 cu. ft.

PROGRAM
Office building for the Department of Water Management and Transport in the province of Zeeland

This office building responds to an ambitious urban development program that was discussed in 1998 for the outskirts of Middelburg. This medieval city needed to have more prominence in the geographical landscape of the Netherlands. The plan consisted in developing the southern part of the city, which was isolated from the rest of the city, save for a canal and rail link. A number of buildings were erected along the canal, which brought about a shift in the border between the city and the countryside. Thus, the project for new offices for the Department of Water Management and Transport saw the light of day within this framework and is one of the buildings that form part of the new architectural landscape. The clients wanted a design that would be functional, transparent in all respects, accessible to everyone, sustainable, and, above all, extremely flexible. It was necessary to have a building that would harmonize with urban development planned for the southern part of the city.

The most important aspect of the structure of the building is its horizontal nature. It runs parallel with the canal, thereby providing a view of the canal and its surroundings

for the enjoyment of its occupants. Both the scale and also the use of the long rectilinear glass as a building material contrast with the ancient buildings of the medieval town. This contrast is a direct reflection of the Dutch countryside, characterized by small medieval villages and designed with fields and orchards in mind, in contrast to the horizontal nature of the long, straight lines of the navigable canals. The architectural construction is elevated above ground, and supported by enormous pillars. This circumstance allows an open area at ground level to be created providing sufficient space to park cars underneath the building and on the triangular-shaped piece of land in front of it. The facade consists entirely of glass, allowing the natural light to penetrate, as well as showing what is going on both in and outside the building. As the client wished, the design's clarity and transparency reflect and demonstrate the fact that important decisions are not taken behind closed doors, but with the clarity and accessibility that information affords.

The office provides work for 450 employees and houses a topnotch computer center. In

an emergency, it can open and close all the sluice gates for the canals in the province of Zeeland. The building also houses state archives, a restaurant, a conference center, and a fitness center. The ground floor is completely open to the general public, while the remaining area is reserved for government offices. The most flexible construction methods have been used for building, using modular components which mean that none of the installations (electricity, telephone, etc.) exceed 3.9 ft., following the grating on the facade of the building. This is another example of a flexible building, permitting multiple internal divisions and a facility for change in keeping with the wishes of the office workers. The fact that it is set in a park encourages meetings, integration and communication amongst the workers, and allows them to enjoy the outdoor scenery surrounding the building so they are in direct contact with nature.

This new office block is a clear example of how savings can be made through the re-utilization of energy by making use of so-called passive solar energy, the climate facade, auri-

cles, heat storage and a cold-water storage system underneath the flooring, the use of active cement. It is a sustainable building that uses materials and techniques that have continued to develop in the international world of architecture to achieve greater economic savings and at the same time, protect the environment by reducing their ecological footprint. These novel techniques mean that the energy generated and stored inside the building is sufficient and not bound to the economic feasibility of the construction. One of the most exceptional and innovative solutions that has been used is the material known as active concrete. This is a new, economical technique in the use of energy, which creates a pleasant, comfortable atmosphere inside the building through the use of 11.8-inch thick prefabricated flooring, inside of which is a system of pipes for the circulation of cold water. This system absorbs heat from the atmosphere and cools it down, so that the temperature inside is always the same. In comparison with the conventional system, such an innovative system leads to between 40 and 50 percent energy savings.

In this office building it was decided to promote horizontal rather than vertical construction, despite the fact that the structure has five stories. By doing so, the architects wanted to reflect the contrast existing in the Dutch countryside, characterized by the unevenness of the fields and the straight lines of the canals. The facade is completely glazed, with long, straight glass panels, allowing natural light to penetrate and making it easy to see the activities of the office workers inside the building.

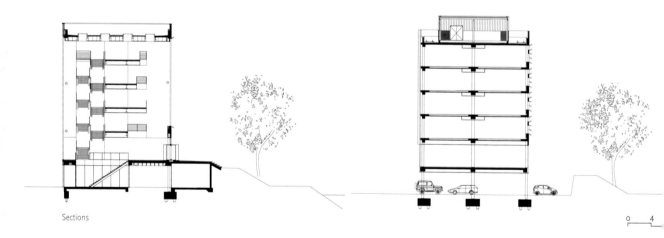

Sections

0   4

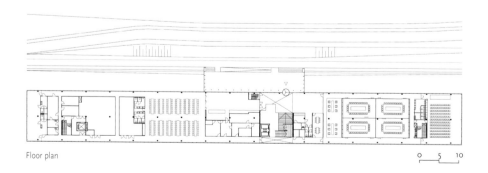

Floor plan

0   5   10

The building is elevated above ground and supported by enormous straight pillars, in keeping with the design of the facade. This structure provides an open area at ground level below it. This level is reserved for employees to park their cars, although they can also do so on the triangular-shaped piece of land in front of the building. The materials most frequently used for the interior decor are wood and stainless steel, which lend the place the degree of harmony and comfort required.

Photo © Òscar Garc

Agbar Tower

Barcelona, Spain   2004

ARCHITECT

*Ateliers Jean Nouvel; Fermín Vázquez/b720
Arquitectos*

CLIENT

Grupo Agbar

PARTNERS

*U.T.E. Dragados, EMTE, Permasteelisa
(constructors); Layetana Inmuebles (promotor);
R. Brufau & A. Obiol (structure); Gepro
(installation); Xavier Ferrés/Biosca & Botey;
Gerardo García Ventosa; Argos Management*

CONSTRUCTED SURFACE AREA

*Building height: 466 ft.
Floors: 35
Total surface area: 511,286 sq. ft.
Below ground level: 188,368 sq. ft.
Above ground level: 322,917 sq. ft.*

PROGRAM

*Building for the headquarters of the Agbar
Group (Barcelona Water) and Auditorium*

Today, the Agbar Tower has become a landmark for the population of Barcelona. Located in the Glòries Catalanes Square, with a total of 35 floors and a height of 466 feet, this building has brought about a change in Barcelona's new skyline. With its use as the corporative headquarters of a water company in mind, architect Jean Nouvel created a small skyscraper, which emulates a jet of water with constant and perfectly stabilized pressure. The architect has created what looks like a geyser surging from the depths of the earth and arriving at the blue sky of the city and has drawn on the architectural legacy of Gaudí and the mountains of Montserrat. The building lies in a hole that surrounds the base of the tower, and not at ground level as would normally be the case. The main construction materials are 891,000 cu. ft. of concrete, one-quarter ton of steel, and 59,619 sheets of transparent and translucent glass. There are 4,349 openings in the structure and 4,500 windows with 40 different colors used.

The constructive architectural form develops from two nonconcentric, oval cylinders capped with a glass and steel dome. On the interior cylinder is the vertical circulation via stairs, service elevators, public elevators and installations distributed on different floors. Most of the elevators are interrupted on floor 26. At the base, three technician floors have been inserted; these are evenly distributed. Four floors situated beneath ground level occupy the entire site and are for parking and auxiliary functions. In the first basement we find the 350-seat auditorium. Between the central axis and the oval exterior are the thirty-one open-plan floors without interior pillars. The exterior wall follows a pattern of one foot; nearly square modules, which have irregularly distributed spaces for windows, create a structure that is dependent only on the precise accumulation of structural tensions, the flexibility of the offices, and the solar radiation. A first skin covers the concrete wall with aluminum sheeting lacquered with 25 different colors of earthy tones, blues, greens and grays that break down as they rise up the building. This chromatic pattern is no coincidence, since at the base the red tones simulate the earthy colors of the floor from where the greens emerge followed in the end by blues in the upper floors like the Mediterranean sky.

The second exterior cylinder stretches straight up to the 18th floor where the structure starts to bend inwards, diminishing gradually before reaching floor 26. On this floor, the concrete comes to an end and a metal structure has been created that forms a glass dome. Here are the last six floors, used for company management.

The entire building is covered with a second skin formed by sheets of transparent and translucent glass, separated from the main structure by 30 inches and supported by aluminum transoms hanging from cantilevered beams fixed to the concrete wall. This allowed the creation of metal walkways on each floor giving access for the cleaning and maintenance of the building. The glass sheets have different degrees of transparency and blur the colorful facade. Their positions are a result of a thorough investigation into the incidence of the sunlight. There are also temperature sensors on the exterior that regulate the opening or closing of the glass blinds, reducing the consumption of energy needed to control the temperature.

One of the building's most notable features, apart from being the third highest structure in the Catalan capital, is the nocturnal lighting. More than 4,000 LED light sources generate illuminated images on its facade, which is distinguishable from any part of Barcelona and from the air.

Gaudí's modernist architecture and the mountains of Montserrat were the inspiration for architect Jean Nouvel when he designed the Agbar Tower. It is like a geyser surging powerfully from the earth and arriving at the blue sky of this Mediterranean city. The color blue is the star, linked with the sky and water.

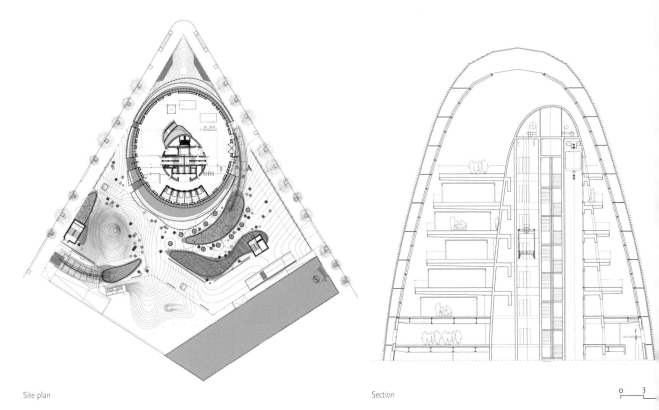

Site plan

Section

0   3

The auditorium, with its 350-person capacity, is situated in the first basement. Due to the undulating topography that configures the open space around the tower, the surface area looks like a hill. The interior design, in shades of red, follows the exterior color range, simulating the earthy colors of the floor.

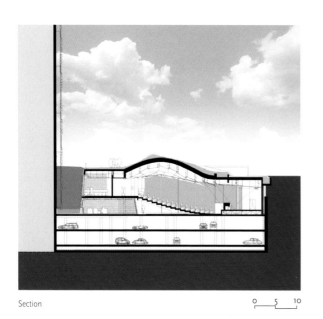

Section

0   5   10

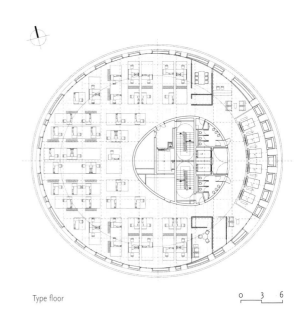

Type floor

0   3   6

Photo © Doug Snower, Miuzhijang Yangqitao, Chen Bairor

Shanghai New International Expo Centre

Shanghai, China   2001

ARCHITECT
Murphy/Jahn

CLIENT
Shanghai New International Expo Centre Joint Venture, Shanghai Pudong Land Development Company, Messe Munich, Messe Düsseldorf, Hanover Fairs

PARTNERS
Hong Kong Construction Holdings, Shanghai No. 3 Construction Co. (contractors); Shanghai Modern Architectural Design Group Co. (designers); Werner Sobek Ingenieure (structural engineering); Transsolar Energietechnik (MEP consultant); Rolf Jensen and Associates (occupational hazards consultant)

SURFACE AREA
3,229,170 sq. ft.

COST
100 million euros

PROGRAM
International exhibition center, restaurants, banks, post office, finance centers, advertising agencies

For the first time in one of the leading Asian countries, an expo center has been created with universal appeal with an international business exhibition program. A local firm took part in this joint venture as the Urban Development Company of Shanghai Pudong with three German companies that organize and run the trade fairs of Munich, Hannover, and Düsseldorf. This expo center was designed for use as a meeting place for setting up highly successful business contacts. The precinct is strategically located in Pudong, the district that has undergone the greatest amount of economic development in the city, to the east of the River Huangpu and just a few miles from the International Shanghai Pudong Airport. The fact that this complex oriented towards international business has been erected in Shanghai is due to this city being the most significant economic, financial, and industrial hub in China, and also the most dynamic. A center of development of the first magnitude, thanks also to the fact that it is in a privileged strategic location, it is the natural outlet to the sea for the wealthy provinces of Jiangsu and Zhejiang, home to more than 120 million people.

The American architects in charge of the design and structure of the complex developed a project with a markedly urban personality. The interior layout is organized as if it were a mini-city, in which the aisles form a triangle with alternate entrances on two sides. Surrounding the building are the covered arcades that link up these entrances with all the aisles. The repeated structures of the aisles create a type of soft undulating design on the roof, giving it character and also providing a symbol that identifies the whole complex. Inside are the exhibition halls, financial centers, post offices, banks, restaurants, customs offices, advertising agencies, shipping agencies, conference rooms, etc. At present, the SNIEC has 18 foyers totaling an area of 1.1 million sq. ft., as well as the 1.1 million sq. ft. of ground outside in the open air. On the northwest corner a circular tower was erected that became the main entrance to the precinct. Next to the exhibition area, there is an office building and a hotel with 400 rooms. Construction was completed in two phases. In the first phase, four exhibition aisles were built next to the outdoor exhibition area together with an entrance. In the second phase, five

exhibition aisles of a taller height were built. This continued in the same way until the current layout was obtained. Each distribution is exactly the same as the others: for example, each exhibition aisle has a covered area of 630 by 262.5 ft. and is supported by 16 columns. The entrance to the hall measures 118 by 262.5 ft. and rests on three columns. The building is supported by a network of intertwining beams that act as if they formed a single structure measuring 236 ft. and protruding at both ends. The longest axis of the protrusion is assembled with structures welded in the shape of a wing to take the weight of the building. The intertwined beams generate rhomboid shapes measuring 39.4 ft. in width and 19.7 ft. in height in the middle. The joints between the beams are strengthened with steel pipes. On the roof, the areas that protrude are fixed with metal cladding and the sections in the center by means of a pretensed membrane made of PVC-polyester. This lets soft, diffuse natural light into the exhibition areas. There is cladding on the internal surface of the membrane that reduces the transmission of heat to the area inside and improves the temperature in the exhibition

halls. The entire structure is supported by tubular columns 46 ft. in height. This horizontal support is reinforced by structures fitted to each of the 4 walls. A decentralized air-conditioning system has been devised for the comfort of the users in the various exhibitions even when there are adverse weather conditions outside. This system is composed of 28 units distributed at 39.4 ft. intervals, which capture the air from outside and cool or heat it depending on what is needed to achieve an optimum distribution of air. The air is renewed by means of 5 extractors that are oriented to extract the air through ventilators located on the long sides of the building. The advantages of this type of decentralized air-conditioning system are its swift distribution of air, its low-cost installation and the fact that it is easy to maintain.

The architects combined concepts such as minimalism, clarity and efficiency in developing this project. The SNIEC is one of the most impressive international meeting points in the Asian Pacific region in terms of aesthetic design, being efficient for its conceptual clarity and functional because of its layout and the size of the exhibition area.

The architects drew up the design of the conference center with a decidedly urban flavor. The internal layout is conceived and organized as if it were a small town. What characterizes the precinct aesthetically is its roof, formed by soft undulations, providing the symbol that identifies the exhibition complex.

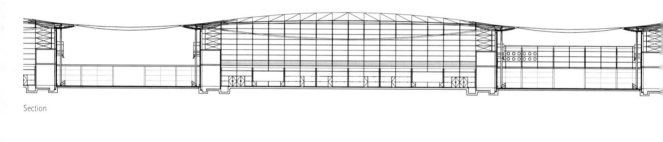

Section

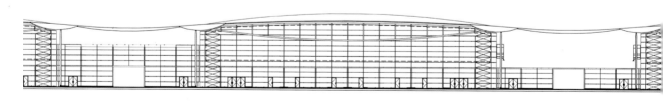

Elevations

0   20

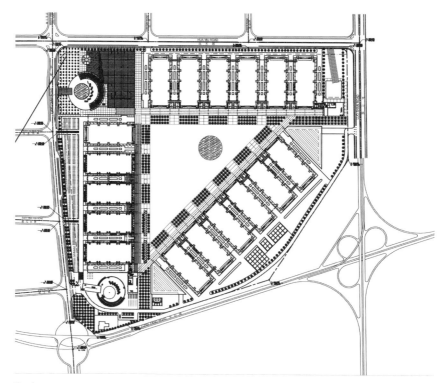

Site plan

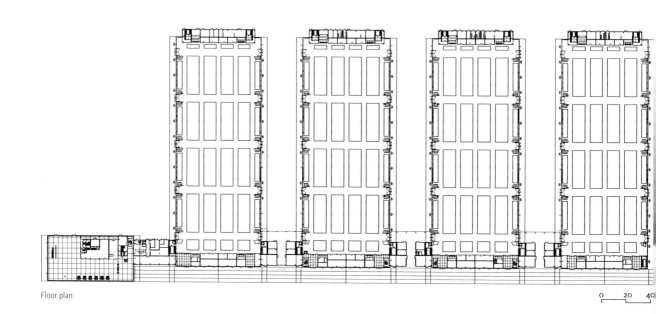

Floor plan

0   20   40

Laakhaven Complex

The Hague, Netherlands   2004

ARCHITECT
Dick van Gameren, Bjarne Mastenbroek/De Architectengroep

CLIENT
Fortis Vastgoed Ontwikkeling NV Centacon

PARTNERS
Corsmit Raadgevend Ingenieursbureau (building); Technical Management Amersfoort (installation); BBF Bouwbedrijf Friesland (contractor); Graziosi Progetti (interior designer)

SURFACE AREA
Offices: 376,740 sq. ft.
40 apartments: 37,670 sq. ft.
Shopping mall: 10,760 sq. ft.

VOLUME
7.6 million cu. ft.

PROGRAM
Building for offices, apartments, and shopping mall

The urban development project, bordered by the Waldorpstraat and Leeghwaterkade, is characterized by the fact that it combines a number of functions. Amongst these are 376,740 sq. ft. of office space, 40 individual apartments, and a wide range of retail outlets. The precinct is located in the third most densely populated city in Holland, about 34 miles southwest of the capital, Amsterdam. The city is currently the official residence of the monarchy and seat of the nation's government, and home to embassies and various international organizations, such as the International Court of Justice, for example, and Europol. Historically speaking, with respect to architecture, the city is famous for the majesty of its institutional buildings and royal palaces. It has an open-plan urban network, with wide avenues and an abundance of parks and public gardens. Over the years, this city has become a place where important cultural events are born, such as museums, theaters, concert halls, restaurants, etc. The district where the Laakhaven Complex is sited used to be an old industrial area, but has now been converted into residential areas and office space.

All the structures forming part of the complex are framed in glass both on the roofs and external facades. This glass envelope indicates the maximum limits of the precinct and functions as a container for the spaces in its interior. The different functions are distributed in various ways inside the building as separate objects. The offices were accommodated in several blocks of varying height, orientation and facade design, whereas the 40 apartments in the complex are accommodated in two blocks with views of the water of the Laakhaven. As an exceptional case, the apartment balconies extend out over the glass envelope, and act as a vantage point for admiring the views offered by the lake and external surroundings. All the volumes in the complex are elevated above ground level; there are no levels underground, and the areas reserved for public and collective use are located between these buildings, these being: a public walkway, an atrium with free access, shops, collective facilities for offices, and restaurants destined both for workers and for the general public. The structures designed for collective use provide places that are suitable for meetings, facili-

tate the relationship between the activity of the complex and its surroundings, and lessen the aesthetics of apparent self-containment of the precinct.

With respect to the interior design, horizontal lines prevail over vertical, with the blocks being no higher than seven stories and distributed in linear fashion, with a predominance of rectangular forms. All the facades have the same distribution with their windows organized in groups of three. This order is occasionally altered by the position of small balconies, which are also glazed but remain in keeping with the overall appearance of the building. The steel girders, which provide the mainstay for the glass envelope, are left exposed. The most frequently used building materials in the complex are glass, which is employed in the structure surrounding the precinct; wood, for the frames on the doors, windows and handrails in the corridors and on the stairs; and steel, for the girders and panels on the facades of the building. However, the material that prevails over all the others is glass, which is used as a handrail in walkways between buildings, for the windows, in a translucent version for the

artificial lighting studding the ceiling, for the railings on the balconies, and in the external structure surrounding the entire precinct. This glazed structure of huge dimensions allows natural light to penetrate directly through the main facades of the building and also through the roof. Such an abundance of direct sunlight means that there is hardly any need for electric lighting and the offices, restaurants, and collective areas in general are afforded the peace and quiet, comfort, and tranquility required during working hours and leisure time.

It is no surprise that the team of architects drew their inspiration from abstract art for the creation of these areas, since it cannot be forgotten that the greatest exponent of this artistic trend was the Dutch painter, Piet Mondrian. His theories of abstraction and simplicity changed the course of art history and had a direct and profound influence on architecture, industrial design and graphic arts. The radical simplification of form and the angles between horizontal and vertical straight lines, along with the use of primary colors such as white, yellow, blue and red inside the building suggest that this style exerted a strong influence.

The precinct, composed of various structures, is characterized by the fact that it is home to a combination of several different functions. Inside, the layout has been designed to accommodate offices, a block of individual apartments, and a wide range of retail outlets for use by the general public. The architects relied on the use of horizontal and vertical lines, right angles, and primary colors to give the environment a sense of balance and tranquility.

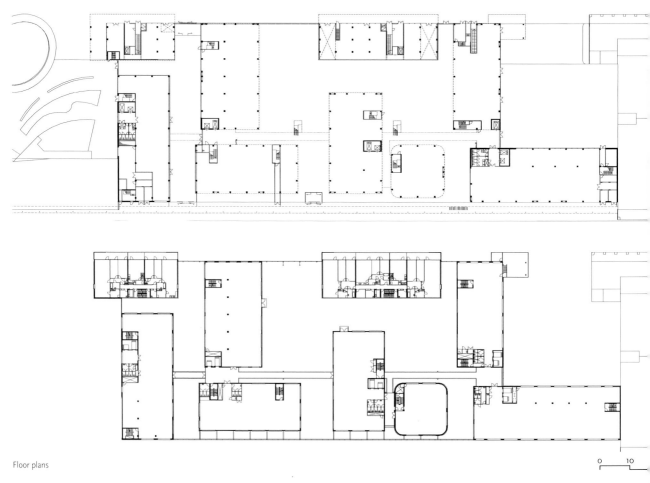

Floor plans

0   10

The different areas are all framed by a glass wrapping that envelopes them and indicates the maximum limits for the urban development project. It houses a variety of functions that are distributed in several different blocks, varying in height, form, orientation, and facades. This glazed structure is supported by steel girders, offering a view of their horizontal framework inside the roof and their vertical arrangement running from street level to the top of the building.

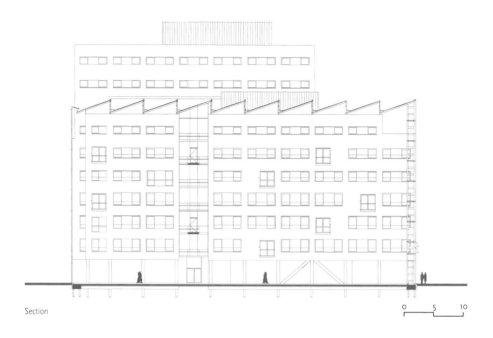

Section

0   5   10

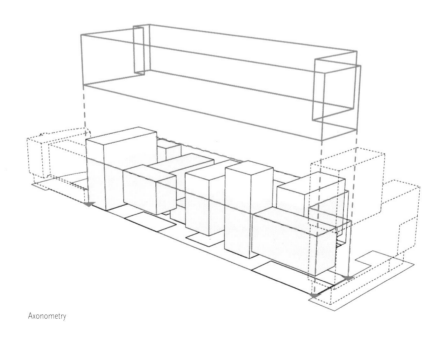

Axonometry

Photo © David Fr[...]

FREMM

Murcia, Spain   2004

ARCHITECT
Vicente Martínez Gadea

CLIENT
Federación Regional de Empresarios del Metal de Murcia

AREA
129,167 sq. ft.

PROGRAM
Training center consisting of a total of 111,084 sq. ft. of usable surface, divided into 11 training workshops, 16 classrooms, a garage with space for 267 cars, a cafeteria, a lecture hall, and small offices

The Antón district in Murcia marries tradition with modernity perfectly. This district consists of two distinct areas: Seda Park, the lung of the district, and the avant-garde church of San Francisco Javier.

This area, a mix of contemporary features and standard buildings, was the site chosen for the building of the Federación Regional de Empresarios del Metal de Murcia (FREMM), a regional organization of employers in the metal sector (production, marketing, repairs, installation and maintenance) established in 1977, whose main function is the administration and defense of the sector's economic, social, and professional interests.

After a thorough study, it was decided to erect the building on the edge of the Antón district to avoid breaking the visual structure of the city center, consisting of buildings given over to dwellings. The site chosen was an industrial estate, and the building stands out from everything surrounding it because it is a modern structure that seamlessly blends with the classic industries established years before in this zone. The building is characterized by its structure

consisting of a large block of concrete in which horizontality is the key. Particularly noticeable is how narrow it is, which gives the building a look of lightness.

Concrete, currently the most resistant material on the market and seen in all types of construction, has the drawback of being considered an overly cold material. It can implicitly lead people to think of this type of building as something distant, while visually it is not in principle an attractive or pleasing material.

Thus, the architect decided to face the building entirely. Although the concrete is still visible on the rear and on one of the sides, it has been painted to give these facades a warmer look; a light shade of beige is used, suggesting simplicity and freshness and increasing the sense of spaciousness. As for the main facade and the remaining side, Vicente Martínez Gadea decided to face the concrete entirely with a framework consisting of steel and glass.

These materials provide the building with different textures while giving it this architect's typical personal touch. His idea was to build a facade with plenty of windows

ventilated by an auxiliary aluminum structure. Because this is a training center (a teaching establishment) the use of glass is an important factor. The interior of the building needs to be perfectly lit and the best way to achieve this is with natural light. For this reason, the whole main facade is covered in glass; to prevent overheating and reflections, a complementary structure has been erected: a steel and aluminum framework installed just in front of the main facade. This structure, consisting of interlinked individual panels, is supported by five concrete columns, and it helps to break up any austerity the building may have.

The architect was commissioned to erect a building that was basically functional, since, from the outset, the building was clearly to be used for training. However, that did not preclude design and current trends, and the FREMM building perfectly combines new architectural trends with functionality.

In the interior of a training center, lighting is the principal element. To achieve the right quantity of light, several key factors come together in this building: first, the large number of windows that let in daylight; second, the white color on the walls, which increases the sense of spaciousness while reflecting freshness and clarity; and the halogen downlights for artificial lighting, which clearly pinpoint the various spaces in the building.

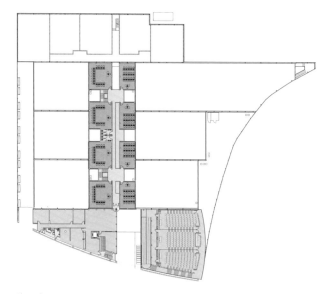
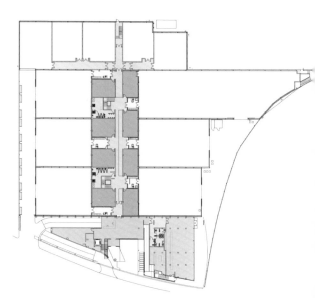

Floor plans

0   5

Photo © Thomas Linkel/Laif, Louie Psihoyos/Cor

Taipei 101

Taipei, Taiwan   2004

ARCHITECT
C.Y. Lee & Partners Architects

CLIENT
Taipei Financial Center Corporation

PARTNERS
KTRT Joint Venture, Turner International Industries (builder); Atkins & Van Groll Engineering (structure); Toews Systems Design (mechanics)

AREA
Overall area: 4.4 million sq. ft.
Built area: 161,459 sq. ft.

COST
Over 1,500 million euros

PROGRAM
Financial, commercial and office building

This enormous 1,667-ft.-high structure, with 101 floors, five basement levels, and a 200-ft. aerial, was built in the capital of Taiwan. It is situated in the heart of the Xin Yi district, a major strategic point; this is the area where most of the stores, businesses, leisure facilities, and residential areas are concentrated.

The idea for the building arose from the need to relaunch the country's economy and tourism, which were yielding ground to neighboring countries. A partnership was formed to take charge of the administration, leasing, and management of the complex. This colossus has put the city on the map, as it is home to what is currently the world's tallest skyscraper. It also incorporates the fastest elevators in the world, another record-breaking feature of this building. The sixty-one double-decker elevators can reach a speed of 3,314 ft. per minute.

The Asian architects took into account the seismic and meteorological phenomena that regularly affect the country, particularly earthquakes and typhoons. A complicated system of seismic resistance was designed to withstand earthquakes of up to force seven on the Richter scale. In addition, a concrete structure was built from ground level to the ninety-second floor, which minimizes the vibration caused by winds of more than 280 mph. On the eighty-seventh floor, there is a spherical pendulum-mass, weighing 800 tons and with a diameter of 20 ft., which is part of a system that absorbs the lateral displacement of the building in case of earthquakes or major typhoons. The exterior facade is slightly inclined to reduce even further the impact of the wind.

The skyscraper's floors are divided into different sections: the five basements contain parking, and the first three floors aboveground contain the main vestibule of the building. The subsequent floors are grouped into three main blocks: lower, middle, and upper zones. The first block comprises levels nine to thirty-four, with floor area varying from 30,250 and 46,285 sq. ft. The middle zone goes from level thirty-five to fifty-eight, with surfaces from 26,910 and 38,430 sq. ft. From levels fifty-nine to eight-four, the area varies from 28,470 and 38,430 sq. ft. The next few levels, up to ninety-four, house restaurants and the observatory. On the

eighty-fifth floor, there is the Diamond Tony Restaurant, serving international cuisine, and the Shinyeh, specializing in Taiwanese cuisine. On the eighty-sixth floor, the XEX restaurant has Italian and Japanese food and a cocktail bar. Finally, floors ninety-two to 101 house the communications equipment. In total, it boasts 2.1 million sq. ft. of office space for 12,000 workers, 834,200 sq. ft. of retail space, a conference hall, and a six-floor annex housing a luxury mall. It is the most technologically-advanced tower in the world; fiber optic and satellite Internet connections can reach speeds of up to one gigabit per second. The whole complex is lit up at night, so that lights forming different angles are projected onto each section.

The building's foundation consists of 380 concrete pillars driven up to 262 ft. into the ground, and the structure is supported on 36 columns, including eight large scale co-lumns on the perimeter. Every eight floors, steel and cement frameworks were added between the columns. All these architectural elements mean that a weight of 700,000 tons of steel and concrete is supported.

The aesthetics of the construction as a whole pays homage to traditional Asian buildings and Asian culture in general. In the building, we see eight elements, the Chinese lucky number that symbolizes prosperity. For example, the original structure of the skyscraper is divided into eight segments, each with eight floors, which give the building symmetry. On each of the four facades, there are four large circles representing the Chinese coins used by royalty in ancient times, and these symbolize good fortune. The glass building in various shades of green looks like a bamboo stalk (a symbol of eternal strength) and is shaped like a traditional Chinese pagoda.

The skyscraper's interior layout was supervised by a Feng Shui expert, who was responsible for finding the optimum orientation to create positive energy flow. Furthermore, the engineers created a new architectural concept: the mega-column. All the steel columns are interconnected in the style of ogives (beams with a neo-Gothic appearance) and come together at a central point as if it were pyramid.

Homes

Bäckerstrasse Apartment Building

Zürich, Switzerland   2000

ARCHITECT
Theo Hotz AG Architekten & Planer

CLIENT
Iwan & Manuela Wirth-Hauser

PARTNER
Jakob Hotz

AREA
24,380 sq. ft.

VOLUME
388,500 cu. ft.

COST
10 million euros

PROGRAM
Luxury apartment building: two apartments, two split-level apartments, one three-level apartment

This complex is situated on the corner of Bäckerstrasse—which gives it its name—and Rotwandstrasse in Aussersihl. From the outside, it looks like an office building, but the long rows of windows and gaps in several places show that the building consists of private dwellings. In addition, it is situated in a residential area, and despite bringing a modern touch to the urban surroundings, it blends in perfectly with the adjoining buildings.

The composition of concrete strips, which mark the division of the floors, and the large windows impose a continuous pattern on the main facades. This harmonious design is is enhanced with the use of the same color on the adjoining buildings. This is why the architect decided to leave the white concrete strips visible from the outside. On the top floor, there are balconies with greenery, which give the building a natural contrast. This horizontal pattern is also transmitted in vertical lines, so that a type of uniform, balanced grid is formed.

The double-glazing affords insulation that keeps the interior temperature constant, thus saving energy, in keeping with the clients' desire to make the building environment-friendly and energy-efficient. The outer layer of glass stops noise and pollution, while the inner layer provides heat insulation. To filter the entry of natural light into the apartments, venetian blinds were chosen to provide privacy.

The residential complex is made of two apartments, two split-level apartments, and a three-level apartment for an art-gallery owner. The spatial layout provides five generous apartments inside. The three occupying the lower floors contain rooms that might be found in any self-contained house on the outskirts of the city. The biggest apartment, situated at the top level, comprises eight spacious areas grouped around a central passage that provides a visual connection between all of them. This dwelling is occupied by the gallery owners who own the entire building. The ordered layout establishes a continuous and seamless sequence between the various spatial features: up and down, left to right, foreground and background, and so on. The stairs have also been reduced to a minimalist design and the spaces are open as in a loft, expressed

with independent volumes that do not interfere with the extension of the space. The patios are linked inside and outside, so that four of them surround what is known as the tower room. This innovative spatial concept is emphasized by the construction materials: concrete as a pure aesthetic material, colored stucco, glass, and wood flooring. The ground level spaces are devoted to stores, another step in the public integration of the neighborhood.

This complex was built in a zone where luxury apartments are not common, and this has become a genuine statement of intent, an acknowledgment of this district that attracts increasingly younger and fashionable immigrants and residents. With this building. the architect has shown it is possible to follow contemporary trends without clashing with the surroundings. He has designed a building that does not copy the aesthetic features of the surrounding neighborhood, but manages to reinterpret modernity and tradition. He has also provided a style characterized by sealing secrets in its interior.

The exterior of this residential complex looks like an office building, but the various features defining the main facades, such as large windows combined with rows of concrete show that the building is devoted to dwellings. The back part of the building continues the same line as that of the facades looking onto the street. An interior community patio with limestone flooring and several tubs with plants and shrubs gives the whole a natural air.

Floor plans

o ⊢———⊣ 4

The gallery-owners' apartment is on the top level of the building.
A central passage gives on to eight different interior spatial areas. The
architect has opted for spacious minimalist areas to create an open-plan
interior. The materials that have been used most are: concrete, manifested
in its purest state; double-glazing, which provides hermetic insulation;
and wood for the flooring, giving warmth to the whole.

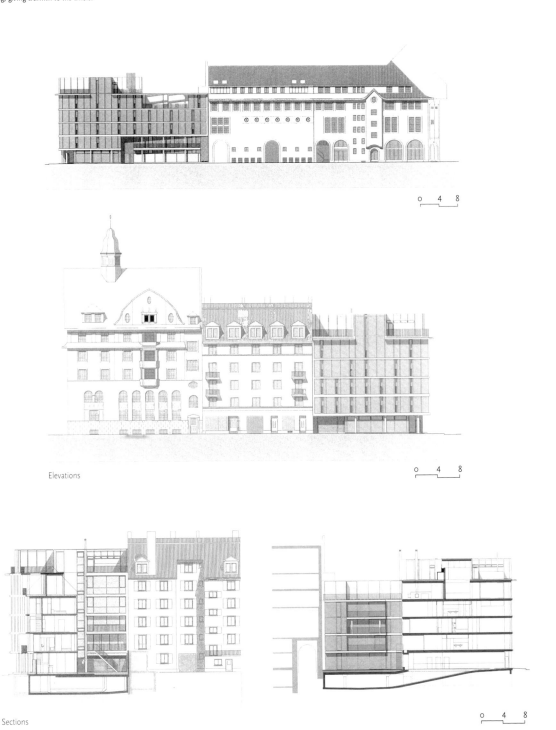

o   4   8

Elevations

o   4   8

Sections

o   4   8

Photo © Ross Honey

150 Liverpool Street

Sydney, Australia   2004

ARCHITECT
Ian Moore Architects

CLIENT
Lion Pacific International

PARTNERS
Infinity Constructions (contractor); Arup & Bonacci Rickard (structure); City Plan Services (planning and building); Arup Acoustics (acoustics); Halkat Electrical (electrics); O'Dor-Out (mechanics); Warren Smith & Partners (hydraulics)

AREA
51,129 sq. ft.

VOLUME
1.63 million cu. ft.

COST
48 million euros

PROGRAM
Building with 35 dwellings

This residential complex is an L-shaped building with three of its facades looking onto the street, in a residential area of east Sydney among high-rise buildings.

Upon receiving the commission, the architects studied the plot and found that it was partly occupied by a two-story building housing a Victorian-style restaurant. Instead of building round the existing structure, it was decided to divide the project into two clearly distinct elements. The main structure runs from the north to the main street in the south part. The second element consists of a square structure that occupies the corner of the neighboring street and part of the extension of the secondary street. The materials and color, as well as subtle changes in the overall architecture, provide the basic differences between the two elements. As far as color is concerned, each block has its predominant hue: the main block is bone-colored, and the secondary, orange. To reflect the visual link between the two elements, three large balconies in the primary block have been framed in orange, horizontal lines predominate over verticals and the rectangle is the

most common geometric feature in the whole. This construction scheme, clearly embodied in the design of the facade, is emphasized by the structure of the materials in chromatic panels.

The most typical elements of the whole are the unusual layout and striking design of the facade in orange. The complex comprises 35 dwellings and has five types of unit, as well as five commercial premises at street level in the main street. The blocks are laid out as two nuclei, joined at the bone-colored hub where the elevator and stairs are located.

The cream-colored building contains most of the dwellings, while the orange block has just one two-bedroom apartment on each floor. Thus, the split-level double-bedroom apartments are in the main building. These apartments cross the main passageway on alternate floors, providing a double aspect and natural ventilation at the intersection.

The single-story one-bedroom apartments occupy alternate floors on the south side of the building. These apartments have balconies that provide views of the residential district and sun all morning. Alternatively, the studio apartments are on the north side

at street level, situated one floor above the basement parking with street access.

Color is the main feature of the interior design. For example, in the kitchens there are concentrated areas of saturated color shades. For this saturation, the standard uniform color range of Vola faucets has been used. Meanwhile, the floors are color-saturated through Pirelli rubber flooring, providing a neutral bone color.

All the facades of the building have been fitted with a system of automatic louvers which are regulated by remote control. This system has a two-fold purpose: first, to control the light directly entering the interior and provide the necessary shade, and second, to ensure privacy from the intersection of Liverpool and Oxford streets in the south. The structure of the main, bone-colored building consists of wall panels and prefabricated and pre-set concrete slabs. Meanwhile, the orange block consists of Vitrapanel slabs made with compressed fiber cement panels backed by ceramic flooring.

The main structure of the project is the cream-colored building. Althoug the building is made of two distinct elements, they are visually linked by three large orange-framed balconies. The position of the balconies provides residents with panoramic views of east Sydney and the benefit of sunshine all morning. A horizontal floor plan is the predominant architectural feature of the entire block of dwellings.

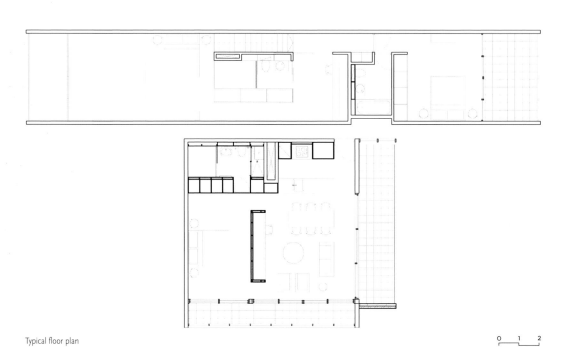

Typical floor plan

0   1   2

In the orange block, the kitchens are concentrated areas of saturated
color with the standard and uniform color range of Vola faucets. The
design is markedly minimalist with light colors on the walls and ceilings,
thus creating spaces that are visually much roomier and more pure.
The aluminum louvers enable residents to control the entry of natural
light depending on their requirements, thereby minimizing the use of
artificial light.

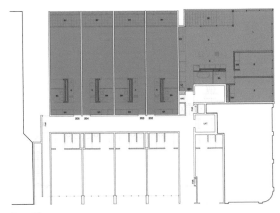

Second floor

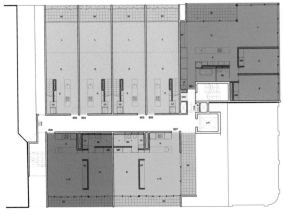

Sixth floor

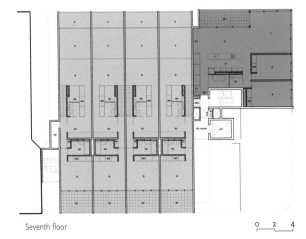

Seventh floor

0   2   4

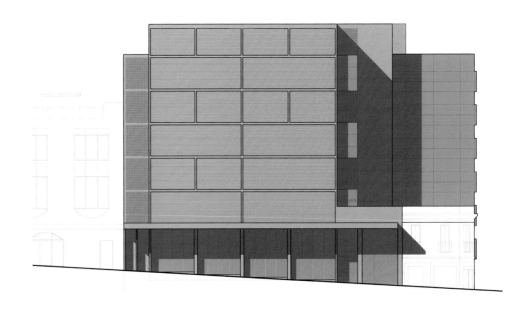

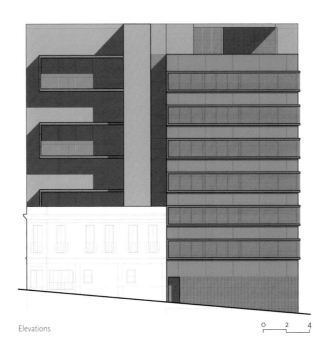

Elevations

0   2   4

Photo © Hedrich Blessing, Steinkamp/Ballog Photograp

Skybridge at One North Halsted Street

Chicago, IL, U.S.A.   2004

ARCHITECT
Perkins & Will Architects

CLIENT
Moran Associates/Dearborn Development

PARTNERS
Samartano & Company (structural engineering); WMA Consulting Engineers (MEP & fire protection); Eriksson Engineering (civil engineering); Ameri-con Enterprise Services (construction management); Walsh Construction Group (general contractor); Wolff Clements & Associates (landscaping); Construction Services Associates (consultant)

AREA
Net surface: 82,800 sq. ft.
Built area: 804,840 sq. ft.
Tower area: 425,440 sq. ft.
Garage area: 379,400 sq. ft.

COST
74 million euros

PROGRAM
Residential tower block

This 430 ft.-high apartment block is situated to the west of downtown Chicago, in the residential West Loop district. Surrounded on the east side by the Kennedy Expressway, on the west by Halsted Street, on the north by Washington Street, and on the south by Madison Avenue, its thirty-nine floors contain 237 dwellings. The site of the building was the criterion for the design, characterized by a balanced architectural composition of the structures to be found all around this building. The result was a dynamic design that attempts to reproduce the fluid nature of the adjoining roads, a design that is not very common in the usual pattern of multifamily dwellings.

The structure of the building consists of a base and a tower that were used as commercial premises for public use and apartments respectively. The linear block runs parallel to the Kennedy Freeway axis in the eastern part, thus maximizing the views of the residential and urban horizon of Chicago. This also helps to reduce the canyon effect that the tower would produce in the western part looking onto Halsted Street. The block also acts as a landmark, since it defines the west-

ern end of the freeway and creates an entrance to the districts west of the Loop that are in constant growth. The 60 ft. base, rising to five stories above street level, is a transitional element between the tower, the developed Halsted Street, and the adjoining districts. The commercial premises were installed on the ground floor: a food store, a savings bank, and a cafeteria. This structure also gives access to the four-level underground parking lot.

The clients and the architects set themselves objectives for the design that challenged the residential pattern of apartment blocks. The design set out to create not a somber monolithic construction but a wide variety of dwellings with different features, combinations, views, and lighting schemes. In comparison with the vertical structure of most apartment blocks, this project called for a thorough analysis of the handling of mass, vacuum, opacity and transparency. These features define the building and are represented in a glass bridge more than 6 ft. high that spans a transparent gap approximately 30 ft. wide. This structure forms an overhanging roof and offers an alternative

vision of the building, as if it were two interconnected towers instead of just one. Furthermore, the elimination of the two units on the fourteenth floor emphasizes this idea of separation of mass and heralds the placing of three additional units on the corner of each level up to the thirty-ninth floor.

The skeleton of the tower was constructed with poured concrete and the exterior with poured glass concrete. The facade was painted in shades that reflected the light and a range of dark gray colors. These gray shades were applied progressively from north to south, setting off mass, shape, and surface. To provide a touch of color, variations of red, yellow, and blue were incorporated, which were used on the recesses and projections of the building; the bridge acts as a connection between the two towers and the upper part of the building.

Another of the features defining the building is the construction of a column that is four levels high, situated on the upper part of the north-facing tower and which supports the open framework of the overhanging flat roof at 40 ft. This is just one more example of the dynamic design that makes it a landmark for the neighboring blocks.

This structural flexibility is also reflected in the interior design of the apartments. Each floor has eight types of dwelling: one, two or three bedrooms with an area ranging between 915 sq. ft. and 4,200 sq. ft. Despite the different dimensions, each apartment has a private balcony affording views of the impressive Chicago skyline.

The original idea for this apartment block was a balanced, flexible and dynamic composition that experimented with the handling of mass by creating empty, opaque and transparent spaces. This meant that a wide variety of dwellings could be built, with one, two or three bedrooms per apartment and dimensions between 915 sq. ft. and 4,200 sq. ft.

Floor plan

0   5

Concrete lends a grayish hue to the tower, and to offset this,
the architects introduced color variations of blue, red, and yellow,
applied to specific areas such as entrances, connections, and the gaps
produced by the original architectural composition.

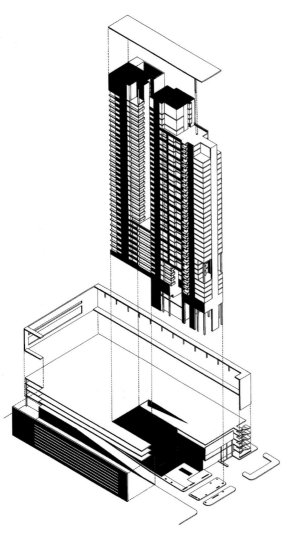

Axonometry

Sketch

Photo © Reto Guntli/Zapaima

JIA Boutique Hotel

Hong Kong, China   2004

ARCHITECT
YOO

AREA
Studio area: 377 sq. ft.
Suite area: 780 sq. ft.
Penthouse area: 1,572 sq. ft

PROGRAM
Five-star hotel with 57 rooms, restaurant, rooftop jacuzzi, outside patio and large conference room

Hong Kong is situated on the northeast side of the Pearl River delta and has an area of 425 square miles, with one part on the mainland and the rest distributed over two hundred islands and islets. Seventy-five percent of this area has large natural reserves, while the remaining 25% is populated by more than seven million people.

Hong Kong is one of the most important cities in China and thus, because of its large population, has become one of the country's major hubs, in the social as well as political and economic environments. For this reason, thousands of business men and women are constantly traveling to this area. These were the circumstances that saw the birth of the project and the idea for building JIA.

The construction of this hotel is special for various reasons: it is the first boutique hotel built in Hong Kong, and it is the first hotel designed and built by French architect Philippe Starck in Asia. The economic importance of the area caused the owner of the building to opt for Causeway Bay, a small district in Hong Kong full of some of the city's most exclusive stores and various entertainment establishments.

When designing the project, the architect drew inspiration from the older apartment blocks built 15 years earlier, in which the interior played a fundamental role and where spaciousness, simple style, and classic lines predominated to secure a relaxing atmosphere. This was exactly what was expected of this building. Its function was to cater to those visiting the city for business reasons. The building would be informal and one could shop there for daily necessities.

Viewed from the outside, it is a building whose main feature is its verticality. The base of the hotel is made of a small square stone structure, subsequently faced with mosaics, that welcomes the guests. The main structure of JIA starts immediately from the base and grows upwards. It is a large block made of stone, a material that is highly resistant to the weather as well as to the ravages of the years. It has a raw color to give a feeling of lightness, freshness, and well-being, typical features of the district where it is built.

The rigidity represented by a building constructed entirely in stone is broken by the

many balconies on all four facades. These small openings give vitality to the building, making it more dynamic and more visually attractive.

The exterior structure is complemented by the use of glass, a material that gives a touch of modernity, class, and elegance to the building while letting in sunlight into the various apartments.

Inside, the main entrance clearly reflects the Starck style, through the predominance of bright, shiny floors combined with curtains covering the walls, contrasting with large plain sofas, marble tables, and African figures as decoration. Structurally, the interior of the hotel is divided into several floors, with a total of 57 rooms and three types of apartments: studios, one-bedroom suites, and two-bedroom suites. Each apartment comprises a dining area, small living area, a kitchen, a bathroom and a small work area. JIA seeks to provide guests with small apartments where they can feel at home, and so it has equipped the rooms with all the basic features required for living. It also provides common areas for relaxation on the large outdoor patio, as well as for business, with a large conference room equipped with the latest technology. The criterion is to provide as much as possible for visitors so they don't need to leave the hotel for something they cannot find inside.

The kitchen areas in all the apartments are fully equipped with all the necessary tableware and kitchenware, as well as a small refrigerator and microwave. Pastel shades predominate in most of the fittings in this area; light colors look clean and help to make the room brighter.

Photo © Radisson SAS Hotel Be

Radisson SAS Hotel Berlin

Berlin, Germany   2004

ARCHITECT
NPS Tchoban Voss Architekten

CLIENT
Radisson SAS Hotels & Resorts

PARTNERS
Wolfgang Wagner (general manager); BHPS Architects, Mahmoudieh Design, Virgile & Stone Associates (interior design); DIFA – Deutsche Immobilien Fonds (investment)

AREA
Different room: 291 sq. ft. and 506 sq. ft.
Suite: 1,087 sq. ft.
Conference space: 14,424 sq. ft.
Relax area: 4,844 sq. ft.

PROGRAM
Five-star hotel, aquarium, car park, swimming pool, sauna, gymnasium, solarium, restaurants and bar

This hotel, whose hallmark is a modern, spectacular design, is situated in the heart of the German capital, specifically on the banks of the River Spree across from Berlin Cathedral. The Mitte quarter, currently the most fashionable in Berlin, includes what is known as the Island of Museums, Unter den Linden Avenue, and the famous Alexander Platz, is the site chosen by the Radisson SAS hotel chain for this new complex. This district had been neglected for a long time but in just a few years it has become the recognized heart that nurtures Berlin, because here one can find one of the world's foremost cultural heritages together with many features that hark back to the past.

The building of this hotel complex has set new standards in the contemporary design of five-star hotel chains. The hotel has 427 rooms as well as several suites including the Nikolai suite, all combining timeless elegance with current modern conveniences.

The hotel's hallmark, the installation of the so-called AquaDom in the lobby, sets it apart from all other hotels. This underwater world, as it were, is an 82-foot-high cylindrical aquarium, the biggest in the world, with

2,500 tropical fish and 260,000 gallons of salt water. This brightly colored ultramodern aquarium was built by International Concept Management, a North American company that came especially from Colorado to install it. The company opted for a contemporary design in harmony with the construction and ambitious architecture of the hotel.

In the lobby, as well as the enormous aquarium, is a transparent walkway made of glass etched with wave motifs. In this setting, the lighting creates an open, friendly atmosphere for the hotel users. These decorative elements, as well as the modular units of the reception desk, the warm-colored sofa in the center, and the original Atrium Lobby Lounge & Bar, all create a welcoming atmosphere. The same design features in the lobby are repeated in the long curved counter of the coffee bar.

The design of the hotel's bars and restaurants puts innovation and serviceability above all else. Also on the ground floor is the restaurant, Heat, which serves authentic combinations of various cuisines, such as spicy dishes accompanied by classic naan bread baked in tandoori ovens imported

from India. The restaurant's name is indicative of the type of food prepared in its kitchen, which has a French Rotisol roaster as well as the tandoori oven. The menu is characterized by a variety of meats and fish cooked in the French style. Another advantage of the Heat restaurant is the opportunity available to dine on the patio with views of Berlin Cathedral. The restaurant's design combines simplicity with the warmth provided by a decor of wood and dark red. The long tables for the diners and the show kitchen enable guests to share the cooking process. This gastronomic concept of modern yet simple cuisine is also echoed in all the hotel's other bars, which serve snacks at any time of the day. A long staircase framed by ice-blue glass panels leads to the Aqua Lounge, one of the most elegant bars thanks to its color scheme, the transparency of the materials, and the water-inspired lighting scheme. Next to this is the Noodle Kitchen, with a ramp leading to the exterior, close to the River Spree. The decor of these restaurants stands out for the Asian elements allied with contemporary features, such as the metal mosaics. The contemporary design of the rooms is marked by warm colors and modern fittings, as well as by well-defined shapes. Here, too, water is the central theme, with motifs from nature on the beds, as well as on the desks and in the corridors. The lighting scheme helps to emphasize this marine atmosphere.

In addition, the hotel has been designed with flexible spaces that can be adapted depending on the conference or meeting. These spaces, next to the lobby, cover an area of 5,705 sq. ft., with a futuristic glass ceiling that lets in natural light and affords panoramic views of Berlin's historic center. The 10 conference rooms occupy in total an area of 14,424 sq. ft. and can seat up to 440 people.

Finally, the building also houses a fitness and relaxation complex, comprising a swimming pool lined with Venetian tiles, a wave pool, a biosauna, and a Finnish sauna, a steam bath and other amenities.

All this makes for a perfect venue that brings entertainment, relaxation, the pleasures of the table and tourism under one roof.

The various restaurants in this hotel complex provide users with the opportunity to indulge in different types of attractive cuisine. They serve dishes based on a fusion of Indian, Mediterranean, and Asian cuisines. The tables are set to enable diners to see how their dishes are prepared at all times. Glass and timber lend warmth and hospitality to the setting.

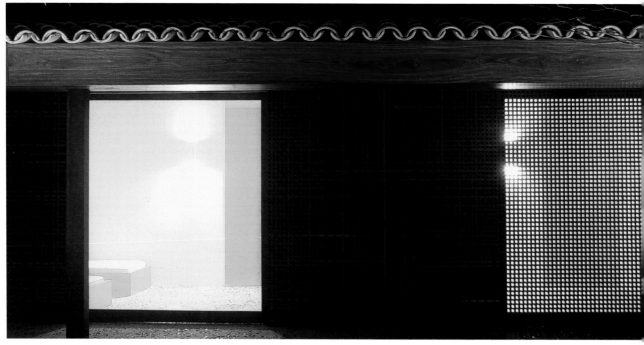

Photo © Arnaldo Pappala

Du Plessis House

Paraty, Brazil   2003

ARCHITECT
Marcio Kogan

CLIENT
Patricia and Alberto Du Plessis

PARTNERS
Diana Radomysler, Cassia Cavan (associate architects); Marcio Kogan and Diana Radomysler (interior design); Bruno Gomes, Oswaldo Pessano, Regiane Leao, Renata Furlanetto, Samanta Cafardo, Suzana Glogowski (project architects); Marcelo Faisal (landscaping); Gramont Engenharia (structure); Fernando Vasconcelos, Alberto Du Plessis, Francisco Vasconcellos (engineering)

AREA
Total Area: 9,924 sq. ft.
Dwelling area: 4,381 sq. ft.

PROGRAM
Family dwelling designed to be occupied by members of the same family

São Paulo is the capital of the state of São Paulo and is the biggest city in Brazil and in the Southern Hemisphere. Considered to be the social, economic, and political hub of the country, it has a population of 29 million plus. Some 250 miles away is the region of Paraty, south of the Costa Verde, between Rio de Janeiro and São Paulo. It is an area of outstanding beauty, with many trails and waterfalls. Paraty is in the Serra Bocaina National Park as well as in the Joatinga Reserve and the Serra do Mar State Park.

This unique spot is where the Du Plessis House was built, amidst the typical lush tropical vegetation of the area.

The owners of this house are a family who wanted to have a private residence that was different from those of their neighbors. The criterion for this project was to obtain two sides of the same coin; in other words, the idea was to combine classic style with the contemporary. The architect commissioned with the project had no problem in achieving this because Alberto du Plessis actively took part in the project from the outset.

The house is a large block built in the middle of a flat area in which the main axis is a patio right in the center. On the exterior structure, there is a contrast between two types of material: the predominant material for the walls is mineira (the typical timber of the area) and for the paving, granite, a material highly resistant to aging as well as to the ravages of the weather.

A preliminary glance at the patio might suggest that the dwelling is fully contemporary, but a closer look into the interior will reveal that a much more classic, conventional decor and style have been chosen. This mixture of styles gives the house a very friendly feeling and reflects an atmosphere of relaxation and tranquility.

The house is a single-story L-shaped structure. The walls representing the longer line of the letter are those that border and define the exterior patio in front of the house, just in front of the bedrooms and the living room which is the focal point of the home's interior.

The house has four bedrooms and in each of them the use of timber is the predominant feature, a basic material specially chosen for the fittings decorating the various bedrooms. The home has been built in an

area with abundant vegetation, far removed from the bustle of the city. Therefore, because of the need to blend in with nature, it has been designed to adapt to this setting as well as to the clients' taste.

Another of the important elements has been the choice of colors. The clients wanted a classic décor, hence the light colors on the walls. These are pastel shades suggesting beauty, purity and spotlessness. In addition, the use of such colors in combination with a material like timber help to inspire a strong feeling of well-being. As far as lighting is concerned, the availability of natural light is a major consideration. Here, the combination outside of cement and light-colored granite reflects the sunlight off them straight into the interior of the dwelling.

The same thing happens with the walls—the typical native timber that has been used filters the rays into the rooms. Thus maximum advantage is taken of the daylight hours; at night, the patio is given a magic touch by the artificial light from fittings in the main areas of the house and a few halogen lights giving off a more direct light through the large windows.

At first sight, it would seem that the dwelling follows a modern design, conceived for a rural setting because of the materials used—timber and stone—and the elements, in this case trees, that have been used to complement the entrance to the home.

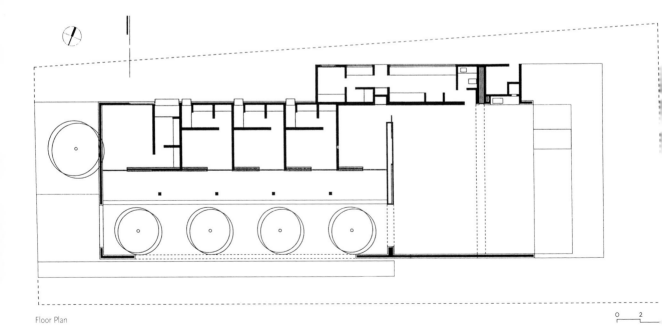

Floor Plan

Photo © Undine P

House in Miravalle

Miravalle, Ecuador   2002

ARCHITECT

Carlos Zapata Studio

PARTNERS

Luis Roggiero Gil (structural engineering);
Moncayo & Roggiero (contractor); Stephen
Christopher Haus, Suzana Perez (landscaping)

AREA

8,610 sq. ft.

PROGRAM

Private house

The house designed by the Carlos Zapata Studio is situated in the hilly part of the city of Miravalle, a settlement that is part of the province of Pichincha, in the Altos Andes region of Ecuador. This region contains the capital, and is the country's tourism center. Because of its broad expanse, it has a widely varying climate and landscape, from desert areas with very low temperatures on the Andean plateaus to the semitropical zones of the western cordillera. Miravalle is known for its mountainous landscape and woodland valleys.

The high mountain location was a decisive criterion for the design. The architects designed a house that would, first, make the most of the views and second, protect and isolate its occupants. The dwelling also had to fully fit in and blend with the surroundings. Two main wings were built forming an angle in such a way that they captured the views successfully, and one of the main facades was glass-fronted to obtain a panoramic view. The main wing ends in an overhanging terrace extending out from the dining room towards the Cotopaxi volcano. This is the highest volcano in the Andes,

with a height of 19,350 ft., as well as one of the most active in Ecuador. The wing at the rear ends on a paved area surrounding the swimming pool and turns into a path leading to the mountain. In the same way as the main wing, the directional axis starts inside the building. The swimming pool, which is partly inside the dwelling, is built so that the bather can take in the impressive views with nothing blocking the line of sight.

The house's construction materials are basically concrete, steel, glass, and timber. The former has been used primarily in the main structure, as well as for the walls and facades. This material gives the unit a more robust appearance, and at the same time increases the occupants' feeling of safety. The facade looking onto the mountain is faced with tinted glass and almost all of it is in shades of green. This material was chosen for this part of the house so that the residents could have a permanent view of the landscape with nothing blocking the line of sight. Similarly, the architects chose the color green to blend the building into the verdant landscape. From the outside one can see the reflection produced by the large

panes, which act like mirrors, and a green tint prevents the interior from being seen during the day. These large panes enable natural light to enter during most of the day, enabling a considerable energy saving. Steel was used for the window frames, on the handrail on the glass-faced balcony that acts as a vantage point, to separate areas indoors, and so on. Finally, timber is the most common material in the interior design and is used on the walls, ceilings, and floors. On the walls, the panels have the same layout as the concrete structures, in rectangular and longitudinal shapes, so that the timber combines naturally with the other materials.

The architects made a painstaking selection of the materials, which blend together; they say that the main objective when drafting a project is to obtain a balance between all the materials. They also managed to integrate the dwelling perfectly into its surroundings.

Wood is the main material inside the house; it is on the walls, the ceilings, flooring on the first story, and the staircase banisters are made of this elegant material, which blends in perfectly with the concrete.

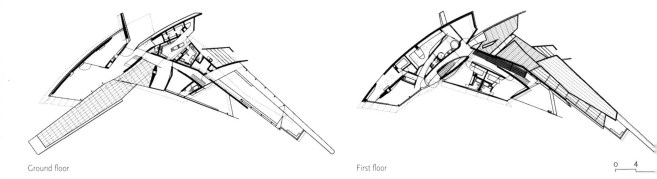

Ground floor

First floor

0   4

The most striking feature of the house is the glass facade that looks
onto the mountain. The glass has been tinted green, affording a view
of the valley from the inside with nothing to block the line of sight.
From the front, the house seems to disappear into the verdant landscape,
while its size decreases progressively.

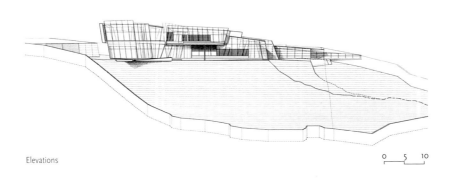

Elevations

0   5   10

Photo © Anton Gra[

May Residence

Brookline, MA, U.S.A.   2000

ARCHITECT
Jonathan Levi Architects

PARTNERS
*Birchwood Construction (general contractor);
Gregorian Engineers (structural engineering)*

AREA
2,000 sq. ft.

COST
195,000 euros

PROGRAM
Private family residence

This private family residence is situated in a town in Norfolk County, on the boundary between Newton and Boston. Brookline's name comes from the streams or brooks that formed the town's boundaries with the farming communities of West Roxbury and Hyde Park, now both integrated into the city of Boston. The town, dating from the 17th century, was originally part of Boston, and was known as the village of Muddy River. It gained independence in 1705, when it avoided being absorbed by the city. The house is situated in a residential district in the southwest zone of the town, a setting characterized by its wild woodland. There is a wide variety of housing in the neighborhood: multioccupancy apartment blocks, row houses, suburban family homes, and large private properties. These typical homes act as a transitional bridge between the outlying districts of a big city and the urban landscape consisting of rows of multioccupancy homes.

As far as the construction was concerned, the architect's first problem was the type of terrain—very steeply sloped. In order to exploit the views provided by the Brookline

hills, the plot was divided so that it was set apart from an adjoining 19th-century summer mansion that blocked the panoramic view. In addition, the two main structures of the building were raised from the ground high enough to afford good views. This meant that the areas of the house that are most used were placed on the upper floors, with the bedrooms at the very top.

The retreat was built to house an elderly couple; their grown-up children all live elsewhere. The clients' requirements were for the architects to build a permanent residence where they could enjoy their retirement. The interior comprises two bedrooms, two bathrooms and a living area. Mrs. May asked the architects for a kitchen that communicated with the living area and for a separate pantry housing kitchen equipment and provisions; this would help her work efficiently. This request was in response to the clients' daily activities, centering on cooking and entertaining. Although privacy was required, the architects installed large windows to take full advantage of the panoramic views in the living areas, and no objection was raised by the owners over this. These large rectangular

windows provide the natural light required to light up the interior.

The structure uses standard components that have been tested and developed to meet residential requirements: hidden sealing and a plywood panel with no joins on the side, providing a natural wood finish. Thus the facade is completely covered with strips of treated timber laid out horizontally. This skin is backed by a rigid insulation that prevents heat from escaping, which is covered by a layer of concrete. This covering also ensures the coolness required in summer and the warmth needed for winter. Such materials mean that the house blends seamlessly into the natural setting surrounding the dwelling. The warm colors used—various shades of brown and black—help to meet the goal of integrating urban encroachment with nature in its wildest state.

The vertical format provides several benefits: it helps create a situation that not only takes full advantage of the space available, but also solves the problem of the sloping land; and it results in substantial savings in construction materials and heating costs.

The main feature of this residence is the structural design marked by horizontal lines that define the materials used on the facade. The treated timber strips are backed with concrete slabs and together they create a thermal layer that acts as insulation, keeping the house cool in summer and warm in the colder seasons.

Ground floor

First floor

0   3   6

Faced with a mature woodland setting on steeply sloping terrain, the architects had to design a structure in which verticality was the ideal solution. The clients wanted to enjoy the views afforded by the Brookline hills, but they also required utmost privacy. Various frames were therefore built up, and the living spaces were placed on the upper levels.

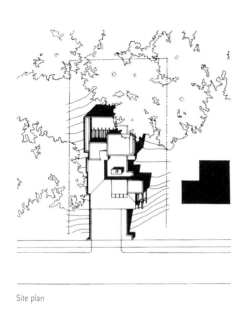

Site plan

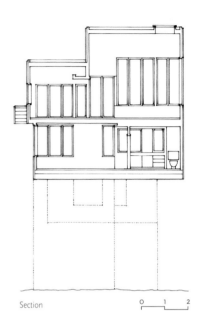

Section

0 1 2

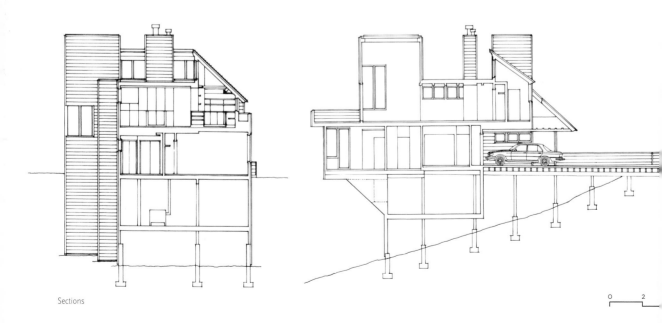

Sections

0 2

Photo © Bruno Helbling/Zapaima

Casa Larga

Brissago, Switzerland   2002

ARCHITECT
Daniele Claudio Taddei

CLIENT
Daniel B. Milnor

PARTNERS
Bianda & Jelmoni (civil engineering)

AREA
2,465 sq. ft.

VOLUME
33,266 cu. ft.

PROGRAM
Studio designed to be occupied by an artist, comprising a kitchen-living-dining room, two bedrooms, guest bedroom, two small bathrooms, basement rooms with show room and toilet

Brissago is a small town situated on the border with Italy, at Switzerland's lowest point, just 650 ft. above sea level. It is a special location between the shores of Lake Maggiore and the mountain slopes. This tract has some marvelous spots that are hard to find anywhere else in the world.

For this reason, Daniel B. Milnor decided to establish a retreat there: a studio away from the bustle of the big cities where he could work comfortably in the sure knowledge that he would not be interrupted. The person commissioned to design and build this house was Daniel Claudio Taddei, a specialist in tricky building jobs like this one. The owner of the future dwelling wanted to place it on the highest point of the hill so that he could have an unbroken view of the lake. This made the job difficult since the only access to this area was, and still is, a small dirt track that can only be tackled on foot. For this reason, the architect opted for a prefabricated timber structure. Split into modules that were brought in by helicopter, the house was installed in three days. The decision to go for timber was governed by the need to design a building that blended har-

moniously with the surroundings, the lake at the front and the mountains at the back. Verticality is the main feature of Casa Larga as it goes straight upwards. It is like a big tower that has suddenly sprung up from the ground and become the highest point on the hill. The exterior of the dwelling is complemented with the use of glass for the large windows, affording views of the landscape, letting in the natural light for the maximum time possible, and providing the studio with the lighting the owner needs all day. This verticality is only broken by a small balcony installed on the central part of the structure. Inside, the space is divided into two floors joined by a wooden staircase. The upper floor is where the rooms for common use are to be found, in other words, the kitchen, bathroom, dining area, and living room. The lower floors is where the private rooms have been installed: the bedrooms, the bathrooms, and the work studio. This is the floor with an abundance of windows because, as stated previously, it is the area that needs most light all through the day.

As far as the facings are concerned, the architect strove to give a touch of elegance

and warmth to the floor as well. Parquet panels have been laid throughout the house and after receiving sunlight throughout the day, give off warmth at night. The only area where another type of material has been preferred is the bathroom; here, rough-textured tiles have been laid to prevent slipping.

The interior decor is dominated by classic, simple lines, avoiding all features that only serve to overwhelm the atmosphere. The most suitable material for the fittings is timber—it unites the exterior with the interior while providing an air of comfort and warmth that is essential on cold days. Good lighting, which is so important here, has also been achieved through the use of color on the walls. Light colors were chosen; pastel shades give the feeling of space and freshness to the home.

The architect has fulfilled his intention, designing and building a home suitable for an artist removed from the world, extremely comfortable and with magnificent views of the surroundings: Lake Maggiore and the mountains.

Building the home at the top of the hill enables the owner to have a magnificent view of the landscape; it also takes maximum advantage of the natural light throughout the day. To achieve this, it was necessary to fit large windows all along the front. The sunlight comes in through them and its reflection on the parquet inside gives the home a distinctive touch.

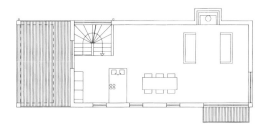

Third floor

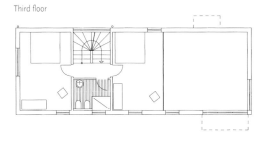

Second floor

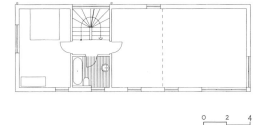

Ground floor

The objective of Casa Larga is to create an environment designed to be used by an artist; for this reason, it has been essential to create a space where he can work without clutter or anything that might hinder his work. He needed a spacious room affording freedom of movement and where there is room for all the elements required to do his work.

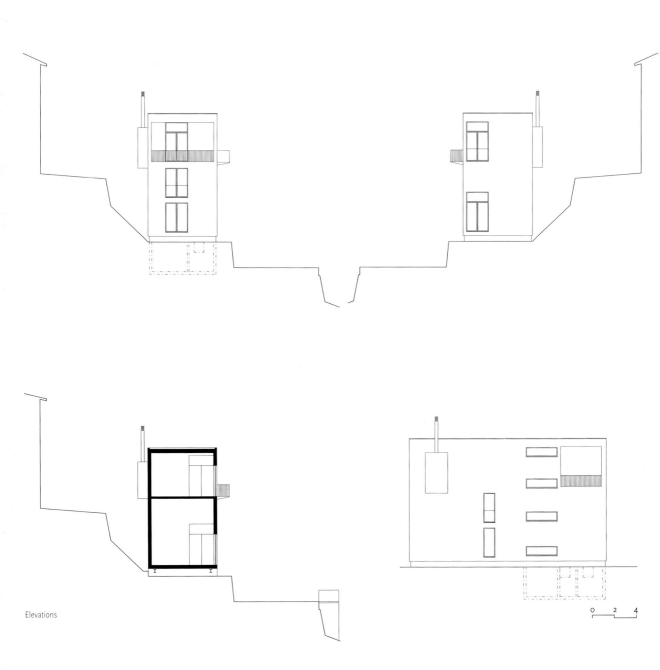

Elevations

0   2   4

Photo © Bjorg Magn

Dancing Bear

Mogollon Rim, AZ, U.S.A.   2004

ARCHITECT

*Blake McGregor Goble/B Space Architecture
& Design*

PARTNERS

Bobby Goble (construction)

AREA

1,991 sq. ft.

PROGRAM

*Private home with two bedrooms and two
bathrooms*

The state of Arizona is known for being the
most mountainous in the United States: a
mountain range runs diagonally across it
from southeast to northwest. Only a few
peaks are over 8,000 ft. high. The Colorado
plateau is distinguished for having some of
the most famous canyons in the world, for
its steep precipices, and for the Colorado
River and some of its tributaries.

All of these natural features make this area
one of the most beautiful in the world and
one of the best settings to escape from the
rigors of daily life. This was the idea of the
owner of this home: to leave the daily routine behind and have a personal space that
would enable him to relax at any time of
the year. This is why he accepted the
design of a specialist in this type of building. The house was built on a flat area of
the Mogollon Rim plateau, some 7,500 ft.
above sea level. The idea was to build a
second residence suitable for occupation
in the summer (as an escape from the
summer heat of the Arizona desert) as well
as in winter (a refuge to relax in after a
long day's skiing at the White Mountain
resort). He also wanted somewhere to

observe the magnificent fauna inhabiting
the surroundings (squirrels, birds, deer,
and even elk).

The home is a large timber structure, the
material chosen to give the outside a natural appearance. The architect has striven to
give the house a life of its own, in other
words, to blend in perfectly with the surroundings so that it looks as if it has always
been there. The strange thing about this
building is that the architect did not design
the exterior first and then adapt the interior
to meet requirements. On the contrary, the
interior was designed first to meet the
owner's specifications and the exterior was
then adapted to what had already been
done. This is why the home's structure is so
striking at first sight—the exterior reflects
an interior space that contracts and
expands, ending up with vast windows dom-
inating the main facade.

In Dancing Bear, most attention is given to
the interior. And here, nothing has been
neglected. The layout of the windows also
had to meet the owner's requirements
because he wanted to see the landscape
before him, with no view of the road or

other houses in the vicinity. The large windows, as well as showing an impressive landscape, admit natural light for as long as possible into the big, double-height living room, where the timber used to create the basic structure has been faced with cedar, used instead of pine, on the walls and the ceiling.

At one end of the living room is a stairway leading to the upper floor, where the main bedrooms are. These open out to the exterior via a large patio-balcony running along the entire back of the house.

Timber is the predominant feature due to the need to integrate the home into the surroundings as well as the warmth this natural material provides. Other materials have been used, too, such as glass (for the windows), aluminum (around the windows and entrance doors), stone, and slate (used to cover all the floors in the home).

The architect has built a second home where the client feels as comfortable as he does in his main residence, the difference being that in this case, the house is used solely for relaxation and leisure.

The use of timber inside as well as outside the dwelling helps the building blend seamlessly into the surroundings. The presence of windows of all sizes as well as the door leading to the balcony make this contact with nature all the more apparent.

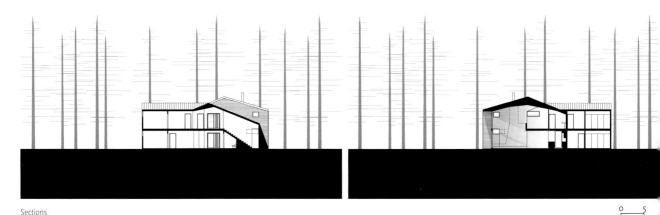

Sections

Tucson Mountain House

Tucson, Arizona, U.S.A.   2001

ARCHITECT
Rick Joy Architects

CLIENT
Kevin Osborn, Robert Claassen

PARTNERS
*Andy Tinucci (project); Rammed Earth
Development (walls)*

AREA
*House area: 2,207 sq. ft.
Porch area: 398 sq. ft.*

PROGRAM
Family dwelling

Arizona is in the American region known as the Sonoran Desert, and in the south is the city of Tucson, which lies in a valley measuring some 500 square miles. It is surrounded by five mountain ranges, three of them with 9,000 ft. peaks and is characterized by its temperatures: mild in spring, fall and winter but scorching in summer.

Here, the client wanted to build what was to be his primary residence. Tucson is not far from Arizona City, so he decided on this peaceful spot with no neighbors, where he could enjoy his leisure time and relax. The building, inspired by the time when the desert was occupied by Native Americans, rises from the ground like a majestic teepee. From the ground up, the home has solid, light-colored stone walls that echo the terrain and enable the house to blend with the environment. The roof is covered with rusted steel in a V shape, to protect the house from the torrential rains that fall at a certain time of the year; its slope helps drain off the water that could, over the years, weaken the building materials. The walls on the north and south facades are each 16 ft. high and more than 2 ft. thick. In the central core,

they go from 11 ft. at the west entrance of the house, to just under 8 ft. in the chimney area on the opposite side. The garage is hidden amidst the vegetation and a small dirt track, lined by the typical cacti of the area, constitutes the access to the home.

The sloping V-shaped roof helps to divide and define the interior layout of the various areas. In the south-facing area are the living room-dining room, the kitchen, and a bedroom; the other area, facing north, comprises the main entrance to the house, a guest room and a spacious porch that links the house to the surroundings. The link between these two areas is the fireplace. Strategically placed openings in the stout walls follow the path of the sun, which as the day progresses moves across the polished stone floors and the texture of the rammed earth walls, marked by the horizontal lines of the formwork.

The construction is completed by the, once again, essential use of glass. This is because it is responsible for linking the interior with the surroundings, and it contributes to lighting the whole building by letting in the sunlight.

The originality of the slope on the roof allows for the subtle, almost unnoticeable creation of various environments inside and outside the house, which establishes a very special combination of settings. The height of the house diminishes in the areas near the hearth, producing an intimate, comfortable atmosphere, while in the areas where the ceiling is higher, the surrounding landscape is drawn in.

Because of its location, the aim has been to blend the house with the desert surroundings. In this respect, the choice of materials for the interior is of paramount importance. The walls take on the same characteristics as the earth outside, since it is constantly echoed in their texture and color. A type of polished stone has been used for the floors in a slightly darker shade to provide contrast, but it also echoes the color of the mountains surrounding the home.

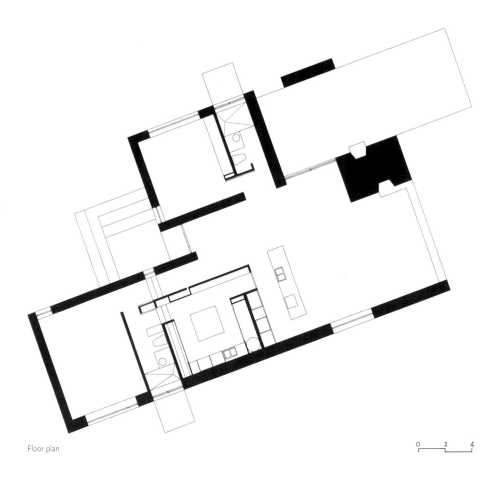

Floor plan

0   2   4

The steel V-shaped roof enables various environments to be created inside the house. They provide the chance to situate all the rooms in common use, such as the kitchen, bathroom, and bedroom in one area, while the opposite end contains an area of complete relaxation, with a guestroom and a small covered patio where one can admire the landscape while being protected from the elements.

Muskoka Boathouse

Point William, Ontario, Canada   2001

ARCHITECT
Shim Sutcliffe Architects

CLIENT
Shanitha Kachan & Gerald Sheff

PARTNERS
*Atkins & Van Groll Engineering (engineering);
Toews Systems Design (mechanics); List
Planning (planning); Suzanne Powadiuk
Design (lighting); Radiant City Willwork
(joinery); Takashi Sakamoto (fabrication);
Judges Contracting (general contractor); Wayne
Judges (principal contractor), Tom Montgomery
(supervisor)*

AREA
1,507 sq. ft.

PROGRAM
*Boathouse designed to be a second residence
with space to keep boats*

The Muskoka region, to the north of Toronto, is one of the area's best vacation spots, thanks to a great variety of activities. There is skiing in winter, while in summer the main tourist attraction is canoeing, kayaking, and other aquatic sports. This factor, together with Muskoka's many beauty spots, make it one of Ontario's choicest rural areas.

Shim Sutcliffe Architects was commissioned to build a second home in these magical surroundings as a family summer retreat. Because they are water-sport fans, the owners wanted a design built on the lakeshore. They wanted it to stretch out before them but also quickly blend into the surroundings. The family specified all the basic conveniences the dwelling should have, in other words, kitchenette, livingroom-diningroom, bathroom, and bedrooms, but the building also had to have an area to house their boats and a small patio leading into the interior.

The design emulated and took its inspiration from three types of landscape: the granite that was left exposed after the last ice age; the pioneers' cabins, in other words, the area's beloved 19th-century cottages and the wooden boats built by local craftsmen;

and the legendary Canadian landscape, which was a frequent subject for early 20th-century artists.

The Muskoka Boathouse structure consists of a single block, and like anything built on the water, the infrastructure is fully submerged. The architects used the typical construction technique of the area, which involved timber framework that gradually made up the structure of the house from the base to the roof. This was subsequently covered and faced with different types of recycled timber joined together using traditional techniques. This type of construction gives a simultaneous modern and classic touch to the building, with the result being a simple, elegant house that makes it the ideal retreat for such spectacular surroundings.

The structure is protected by the roof, made of another framework of different types of timber and faced with smooth aluminum panels, which protect the dwelling from the ravages of winter weather and prevent rainwater or snow from collecting there.

The architecture establishes a very close relationship with the water. The house includes two interior moorings and a cov-

ered mooring outside, which means that the boats are available at any time for a trip on the lake. It also has storage for all types of aquatic equipment, as well as all the living areas required for a dwelling, including a main bedroom, a bathroom, a kitchenette that is connected to the living room, and various porches and outdoor patios, including a moss garden with local species of moss. The structure makes abundant use of glass, essential for this type of dwelling. Because this is a retreat occupied only during strictly necessary times, artificial lighting is of secondary importance here. Maximum advantage has to be taken of natural light, and so windows have been installed all around the building, producing optimum light during the day and a play of light and shadows on the timber that gives an air of elegance and adaptation to the surroundings.

The Muskoka Boathouse layout was drawn on the ice during the winter, when the lake was frozen, thus allowing an early start to the project. The cabin was designed as a sophisticated refuge with a classic interior lined with mahogany, birch, and fir as well as a protective roof made of resistant timbers joined together with traditional techniques, then covered with aluminum panels to protect the home from inclement weather. All these interrelated features, and other contrasting elements, create an almost imperceptible link between the dwelling and nature.

The project was designed in winter, when the lake is frozen over. The layout of what was to be the home and the detailed location of the framework that was going to support the main structure were drawn on the ice. The architects bore in mind that the main function of this building was to serve exclusively as a retreat during certain hours of the day because it was designed as a residence for leisure and relaxation.

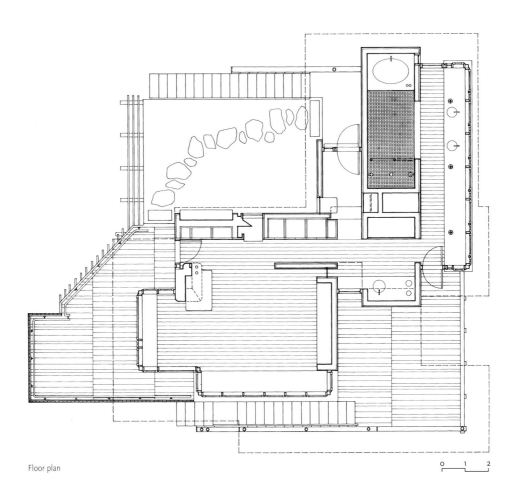

Floor plan

0   1   2

Photo © Paul Finkel, Piston Design, Lost Pines Aereal Photogra

Guest House

Austin, TX, U.S.A.   2005

ARCHITECT
Miró Rivera Architects

PARTNERS
Architectural Engineers Collaborative (structural engineering); Don Crowell (general contractor)

AREA
2,508 sq. ft.

PROGRAM
Three-story family home

This guest house is located on a small two-acre peninsula in the Texas state capital. This city is known for the production of hi-tech equipment, as well as for production of hydroelectric power, and its surrounding areas are authentic natural beauty spots. This residence is on one of these natural terrains of exceptional beauty, and is surrounded by water and vegetation such as rushes. These marshland areas serve as a migratory stop-over for swans, cranes and egrets. The land is reached via footbridge, inspired by the vertical, cylindrical shapes of the rushes, the main feature of this beautiful landscape. To ensure that this urban incursion integrated perfectly with its natural setting, the designers used steel with an unrefined look, folded and oxidized. This tile-colored construction announces to visitors that they are entering a wild, natural setting.

The architects carried out a thorough, meticulous analysis of the existing vegetation and the wildlife of the plot. This is why the architects had 10 years to complete the project, which consisted of removing plants that were the most aggressive, planting native plants, and restoring and extending the existing marshes. Under these circumstances, the house had to be built with as little impact on the environment as possible. The only viable solution was to opt for height rather than breadth in the construction. This way, the architects designed a building that occupied little ground space. The interior spaces were to be distributed in rooms laid out over three floors. The largest floor houses the kitchen, the rooms that receive the most use, and the dining and living areas. This main floor opens onto a patio that surrounds it and is separated from the structure by a glass skin. This original covered platform seems to be floating on the building because the surrounding native plant life camouflages the house in the landscape. The ground-level patio has undulating shapes and is dominated by a vast cylindrical pillar with the same metallic tones as the rest of the residence.

A box-shaped volume of glass peeps out over the flat roof of the ground floor. Here, on the second floor, is the master bedroom, and on the third floor, the other two bedrooms. The areas used during daylight hours which require a large amount of natural light

are in this glass structure. The large windows on the facade have two main purposes: to afford a continuous view of the natural landscape and also to allow natural light to make its presence felt in the interior and create an open atmosphere of total calm. Whenever the house is empty, a screening system with steel frames and timber slats can be employed. This is usually folded away, so that when it is needed it can be opened out to screen off the large windows entirely.

The glass assemblage is joined to another three-story structure that contains the stairs to all the levels of the building, the bathrooms, and the main closets. This module is coated with pinkish rust-colored cooper. It stands out in contrast to the straight, angular lines of the glass structure by creating an undulating shape on its facade that adapts to the requirements of the interior spaces it houses. The metal is laid out in strips that mold themselves and bend completely, adapting to the line of the surface.

The guest house is a safe family home that fully blends in with the landscape. Its unique spatial layout enables the occupants to enjoy the wild beauty of the surroundings.

This residence is situated on a peninsula, surrounded by wild vegetation that camouflages it within the flora of the area. The main feature of its original architecture is a series of structures that, at first sight, seem incompatible, but that mesh seamlessly: a glass boxlike structure with angles and straight lines, and a metallic module with undulating lines.

Third floor

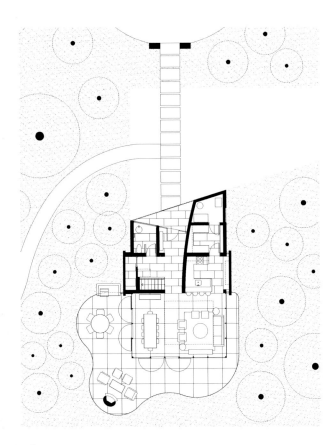

First floor

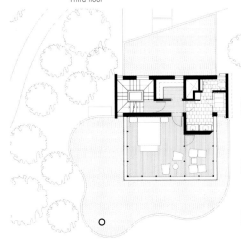

Second floor

Photo © Jeroen M

Sphinxes

Guisen, Netherlands   2003

ARCHITECT
Neutelings Riedijk Architects

CLIENT
Bouwfonds Wonen Noord West

PARTNERS
Bureau Bouwkunde Rotterdam (technical consultant); Ingenieursgroep van Rossum (structure); Coen Hagedoom Bouw (contractor)

COST
11 million euros

PROGRAM
Residential complex of 70 apartments in five buildings

Sphinxes is located in a small town called Huizen in the Netherlands. The country's name, Nederlanden, literally means Low Countries and in fact most of the country is below sea level. It is an area where water plays a fundamental role because most of the land is washed by canals, rivers, and coastal inlets. The dykes, canals, and dams that typify the Dutch landscape are part of a water-drainage system that was set up in the Middle Ages and has contributed to a 20% growth in surface area.

In view of the large amount of water in the Netherlands, buildings need to adapt to the surroundings while taking maximum advantage of them. These were the circumstances that saw the birth of the Sphinxes project. The architects were commissioned to create a residential area that would blend in with the environment, in this case a lake. At the same time, it needed to be a modern, contemporary idea, something that had never been seen hitherto, but which involved no risk of any kind for the inhabitants when they moved into their residences. This residential complex was named Sphinxes because its construction and structure were reminiscent of the shape of the great sphinx that presides over the legendary realms of Egypt. The residential area is divided into five large blocks, each with 14 apartments laid out in such a way as to take advantage of daylight for the longest time possible. The architect considered the personal requirements and tastes the future occupants might have, and decided that all the apartments should look onto the lake. For this reason, the layout of the apartments changes from floor to floor, with each apartment having one room less than the one below it. This succeeds in creating a pyramid structure affording each apartment natural light and a view of the landscape.

The large blocks of dwellings emerge from the lake through a large stone structure that gives the area an air of majesty and makes the buildings seem impenetrable. These buildings take on a stately appearance within their domain and have a great visual impact. An area of stones and reeds helps to filter the water and softens the transition between the shore and the buildings.

To enter the buildings, there is pedestrian access through walkways that also lead to

the garages located underneath the first floor of the apartments.

As far as materials are concerned, glass plays a leading role and predominates through the entire structure, enabling the maximum amount of sunlight to enter. This is helped by the fact that all the patios face south.

An important factor is that the site of these buildings affords views that are unavailable in other parts of the town, since this area has as many as four different elements: the esplanade in front of the ramps leading into the dwellings is a perfect children's play area, the proximity of the sea for water sports, on the lake for fishing, and finally, areas in the dwellings that become large balconies for sitting outside to enjoy majestic views. The location of these sphinxes and the calmness of the waters create a unique peaceful environment.

The lake in front of the buildings gives a marked feeling of vitality to the area. Here, the sphinxes rise up majestically and blend into the surroundings in such a way as to appear as though they emerged from the lake itself. The absence of any other building in the vicinity affords an unsurpassable view and also means that natural light is available for most of the day.

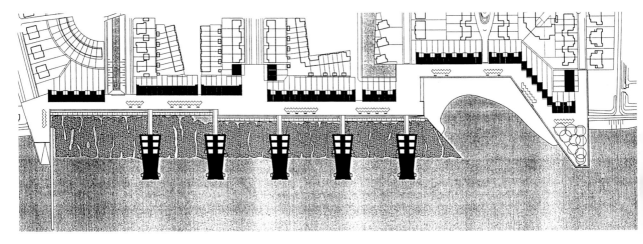

Location plan

Photo © Jordi Mir

Ocotal Beach

Playa Ocotal, Costa Rica   2005

ARCHITECT
Víctor Cañas, Joan Roca/Aquart (landscape architect)

PARTNERS
Joan Roca/Aquart (consultant); Tom Terry (contractor); Skip Phillips (hydraulic design)

AREA
3,230 sq. ft.

COST
196,000 euros

PROGRAM
Family dwelling near the sea

This majestic house is on a mountainside on the Pacific coast of Costa Rica, in a favored position 650 ft. above sea level. This position affords view of the Nicaraguan coast as well as a 360-degree panoramic view. The owner's main objective, as well as the architect's, was to integrate the dwelling into the natural surroundings so as to have as little impact as possible on the environment. Costa Rica has the greatest biological wealth in the world in a very small space, just less than 20,000 square miles. It has 5 percent of the world's biodiversity, and so painstaking work has been done to safeguard the environment by running a broad program based on sustainability. Both the public and the government have been running campaigns to protect and preserve the ecosystem and natural resources of this Central American country.

The architect presented an original and highly innovative design, for which he gathered the country's best architects around him. The result is a minimalist and contemporary architectural composition, in which the house seems to be floating on water. To achieve this, he created an area measuring approximately 3,230 sq. ft.—the equivalent of the total dwelling area—and filled it with water, thus creating the effect of a glass sheet. This structure seems to emerge from beneath the house and extend to an open patio that looks onto the sea, passing in front of the living room, kitchen, dining room, access zones, and main bedroom. The rest of the facades were built on the plot normally. The sheet of water is like a mirror which reflects and faithfully reproduces the silhouette of this family home. So as not to use too much water, the pool has a depth of just 6 inches. This water was connected by means of steps to a 430 sq. ft. area situated in front of the living room and patio, where it becomes an infinity pool whose depth ranges between 4 ft. and 5 ft. This pool blends into the ocean and creates an effect of continuity thanks to an almost invisible edge 130 ft. long. The structure integrates the foundations of the house into those of the pool so that the engineers who built the pool had to work closely with the architects to create a complex hydraulics system.

The inner surface of the pool was lined with iridescent vitroceramic tiles measuring 1 inch-by-1 inch. Black, pewter, and bronze tiles were used alternately, forming a mosaic of gray shades that contrast with the whiteness of the house. This mosaic emphasizes the mirror effect and reproduces a spectacular image of the house. The outer wall of this infinity pool is visible from different angles and was lined with the same material as the inner walls. However, the upper part is painted white to harmonize with the design of the whole.

The outdoor patio is designed in the style of the interior design and its main feature is the cream color scheme provided by the limestone and the glass and metal handrails. The main bedroom includes a second private patio, whose main construction material is teak, which projects towards the ocean over the pool, supported on a metal structure in the manner of a lookout point.

Wooden bridges and platforms were built over the water in many parts of the house, emphasizing the sensation of floating on water. The materials selected to establish direct connections between the interior and exterior of the house were glass and stainless steel; the former was used in the vast windows and handrail structures, and the latter for the support structures.

The spectacular nature of the pool seamlessly blends with the geometric minimalism of the architecture of the house. At the same time, these two main features of the whole respect the natural beauty of the Costa Rican landscape. The favored position of the home affords the owners panoramic views of Costa Rica's Pacific coast.

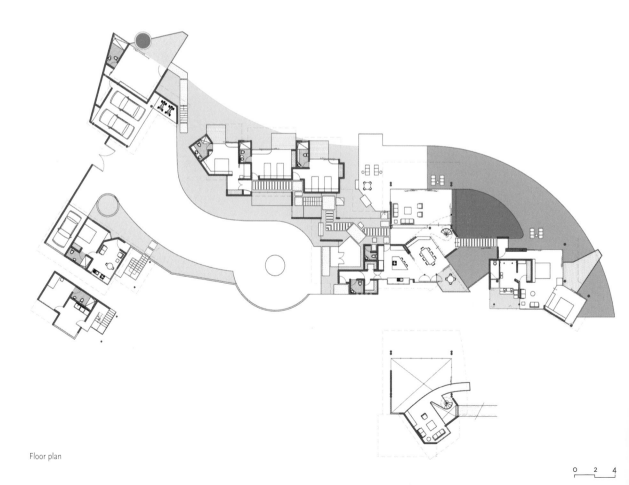

Floor plan

0   2   4

The materials selected for the construction of the house and the pool were concrete, limestone, glass, stainless steel, wood and ceramic tiles, in various color schemes. These materials, together with the minimalist design and the use of simple geometric forms, meant that the dwelling had a very small visual impact on the natural surroundings.

Photo © James Silver

Villa Näckros

Kalmar, Sweden   2003

ARCHITECT
Staffan Strindberg/Strindberg Arkitekter

CLIENT
Modern Marine Homes

PARTNERS
Carl-Johan Svahn, Svahns Konstruktionsbyrå (consultants); K-V bygg, Tecomatic (general contractor); Andrew Gauld (exterior lighting); Olga Thorsen, Källemo, Eva Hild, Kosta Boda, Mora, Bruno Matson International, Zero, Gauld Design, Lomakka, Nordic Light, Svenska Badkar, Åki Axelsson Anshelm, Eglo, Kvänum (suppliers)

AREA
1,916 sq. ft.

COST
639,000 euros

PROGRAM
Floating house

This floating family home is situated in the medieval city of Kalmar, on the west coast of Sweden. This city of some 35,000 inhabitants is known for its trade and shipping and was a major strategic point on Baltic routes.

As with the construction of all floating houses, the design suffers the constraints of space and convenience. A solution based on a dynamic, spacious, and contemporary setting was used to build this residence. The space combines all the luxuries of a modern home with the spatial freedom and panoramic views that can only be had on the coast. To achieve this objective, painstaking planning and careful thinking was required by the team. The plan's success hinged on the repetition of spaces; this simplified the building process and saved costs.

The result was a square building with a 1,916 sq. ft. area, consisting of three half-levels, a patio, and a small roof garden. Because the architects' and clients' main objective was not a floating house that would move over the water, it was decided to do away with the traditional boat shape. This was why a square shape was chosen for the dwelling, a decision that was largely taken because of the need to create a structure that was as stable as possible. The hull of the residence was made of reinforced concrete, treated on the outside to act as insulation and prevent damp in the interior. The weight of the concrete, combined with the structure of the frame, provides the necessary stability to enable the dwelling to be used naturally. Two of the four corners of the dwelling were fitted with deep-red, grooved aluminum sheets, which provide the building with a color contrast, as well as a silhouette that looks striking from the outside.

Another of the objectives met was to make optimum use of the area in order to obtain a space that was comfortable and roomy. The appropriate solution was to create small spaces divided into different levels. The installation of large windows running from floor to ceiling provides plenty of light to the interior and emphasizes the feeling of roominess.

Access to the residence is via a small ramp leading to a rectangular passage. Inside, the kitchen is to the left; it is constructed entirely with stainless steel and oak, practical

materials that give the surroundings a sense of comfort and create a sociable atmosphere. On the left is a stairway leading to a mezzanine floor that contains the study, the main feature of which is large windows providing the natural light required for normal activities carried out in a space like this. On a level below the kitchen, the same stairway leads to the lounge, which one crosses to reach a patio at water level. Downstairs are the rest of the rooms: three bedrooms and two bathrooms. The fittings and interior decor are designed to make the setting as pleasant, comfortable, and sociable as possible. Serviceability is one of the prime requirements for comfortable living. On the upper part of the building is the garden with an area of 1,076 sq. ft.; its location enables the residents to sunbathe as well as to enjoy panoramic views of the riverside.

Every stage of the design is geared towards emphasizing expanse and light. To this end, it was decided to install oak flooring and to paint the walls white, as a way of neutralizing the contrast. The effect highlights both the decorative accessories and the furniture, which are treated as genuine works of art.

Night lighting was also taken into account when designing the interior. The lights were strategically installed at various points of the residence to highlight the outline of the house, as well as to fully illuminate the main rooms.

Villa Näckros has become the prime example and archetype of the water home, enabling savings in the construction of this type of dwelling. It is the first project in a range to be launched by the company formed by the architect and owner of this dwelling.

The first rooms one comes to when entering this floating house are the kitchen and lounge. The stainless steel, the oak flooring, and the neutral walls make the whole a well-lit space with plenty of room. The distribution of the rooms at different levels and the large windows running from floor to ceiling emphasize this effect.

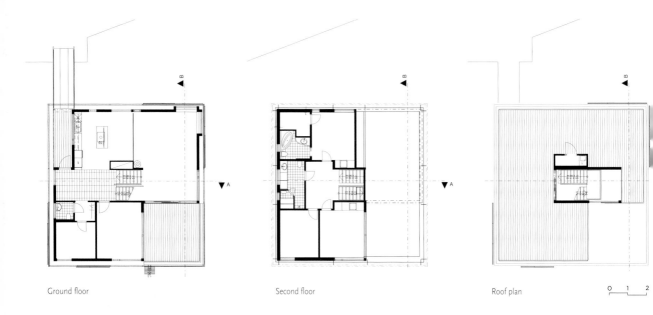

Ground floor

Second floor

Roof plan

0   1   2

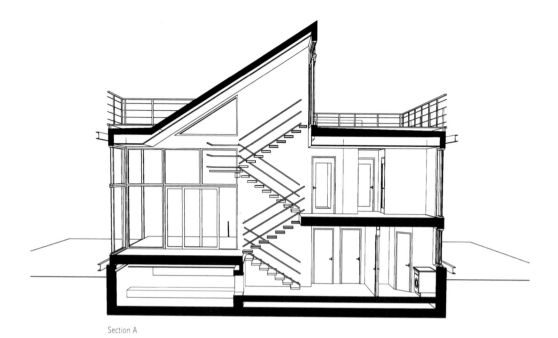

Section A

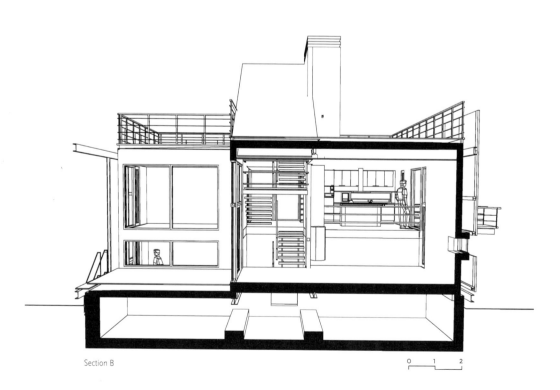

Section B

0 1 2

Photo © Brett Boardr

Arkiboat House

Berowra Waters, New South Wales, Australia   2003

ARCHITECT
Drew Heath

CLIENT
Ian Ugarte

PARTNERS
Terry Dwyer, Daniel Girling-Butcher

AREA
646 sq. ft.

COST
18,168 euros

PROGRAM
Private floating home

Welcome to Australia, home to one of the world's most expensive and inaccessible areas. Thirty miles from Sydney, the legendary architect, Gell Murcutt, designed and developed an area known as Berowra Waters, which can only be reached by a privately run ferry or by seaplane or private boat. The town's most important river, the Hawkesbury, runs through the Cattai National Park, and a stretch of this river is populated by the country's wealthiest inhabitants and rich foreigners.

It is an exclusive area steeped in the comfort and luxury accessible to the privileged few.

One of them, Ian Ugarte, decided he wanted a small house here, a dwelling where he could enjoy a few days' rest far from the city without sacrificing the convenience and comfort that homes should have. He commissioned Drew Heath, who had previous experience with projects of this kind, to design and build the house.

The house sits on a solid surface made of resistant materials that are not affected by contact with the water. This structure is clad in another material, which is what really constitutes the basis of the house. Here the

architect has chosen timber, because it is a material that suggests warmth and because it is not slippery when it comes into contact with water. The design is complemented by a small detail that easily escapes notice but that is vital: a railing that goes all the way around the house and provides security. The composition is a combination of timber (the material that is most used here) and aluminum, which gives it a fashionable air and provides a contrast in a structure which, to this point, has been dominated by timber.

Inside, there is a predominance of timber panels, intended not only to give warmth to the dwelling, but also to provide a material that is well suited to houseboats because of its light weight. Another basic material used is glass, affording good views of the surroundings wherever the dwelling may be, and enabling the vessel to take maximum advantage of natural light. These qualities manage to lend an air of spaciousness to a home that is dwarfed by its surroundings.

On top, the roof is formed by a large sheet of metal. This is larger than the footprint of the house to protect the structure from

adverse weather conditions. The architect opted for metal when building the roof because it is a highly resistant, durable material. The large metal sheet is clad with small white aluminum panels which make the roof more attractive to the eye. Finally, the ceiling is complemented by dim lighting that is used after sunset. The architect decided to install downlights that give off a clean, clear light. He thus managed to avoid large light fittings, unnecessary in this type of dwelling because they need more space.

The dwelling is situated in a natural environment, in the middle of a river and surrounded by mountains and vegetation. For this reason, it needs to be just another feature in this environment. To achieve this, the architect opted for materials such as wood and glass, elements that are warm in themselves and that blend in with nature.

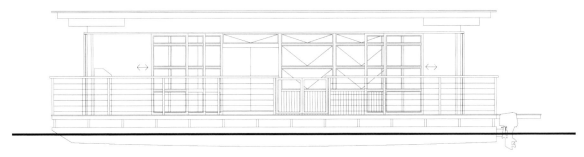

Elevation

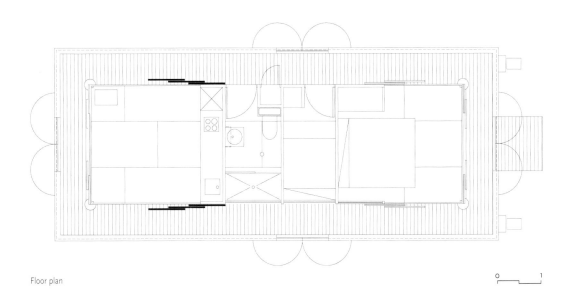

Floor plan

0   1

A space in the open air is a guarantee of large quantities of natural light, and this has to be exploited to the maximum. In this small dwelling, there are many light tones (as seen in the timber), and just one color, white, which suggests elegance and freshness and helps to provide the home with a warm, intimate air.

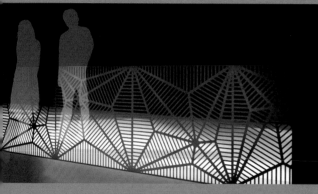

Architecture for the Future

Photo © Softroom Architec

Floating Island

Mobile, Virtual   1997

ARCHITECT
Softroom Architects

CLIENT
Wallpaper *Magazine*

AREA
670 sq. ft.

PROGRAM
Summer residence and artificial floating island

This floating island was designed by a young architects' studio in London, the specialty of which is innovative, high-quality projects. The design proposed here is for a residence than can be transported and established anywhere.

The actual construction of a one-off project would be very expensive; if it were to be put into production, it might be viable. It has been calculated that the total price of a series of mobile, floating islands would amount to the same as the building of a private yacht.

Currently, the main problem in homebuilding is the lack of land to build them on. Other factors, such as spatial density and a desire for mobility also affect the building of permanent homes. The solution is addressed by a mobile floating design, whose location would be the least of any problem. This shelter is a summer dwelling enclosed in a carbon-fiber bubble. One of the faces of the bubble has been designed so that it can be opened easily; it can serve as a stabilizing element for the

unit, it can cover the residence whenever required, or it can function as a patio for the cabin.

Once the bubble is opened, the dwelling appears, and it has the look of a typical beach house. The bed and sofas inflate automatically to provide furniture that is in line with the use of the accommodation. As well as these items, there is also a platform that acts as flooring, a desalinated-water shower, a bar, and seats covered with neoprene.

As soon as the module cover opens, the floating island unfolds, and the surrounding areas are inflated by means of a generator. The result of this self-construction process is what looks like a beach made out of polyurethane surrounded by water. In short, what is created is an artificial setting providing the right conditions for the enjoyment of this type of residence. The convenience of the unit and its ability to be transported has led the architects to consider that this type of dwelling might be the answer to the problem of population density typical of large cities.

Photo © Diller Scofidio & Re

Eyebeam Institute

New York, NY, U.S.A.   2007

ARCHITECT
Diller Scofidio & Renfro

CLIENT
Eyebeam Museum of Art and Technology

PARTNERS
*Charles Renfro, Deane Simpson, Dirk Hebel
(projects); Ove Arup (structure & MEP
engineering); Helfland Myerberg Guggenheimer
(associate architects); Ben Rubin, Tom Igoe,
Joe Paradiso (consultants); Mueser Rutledge
(engineering); Joshua Bolchover, Alfio Faro,
Reto Geiser, Gabu Heindl, David Huan, Dieter
Janser, David Ross (additional team); Matthew
Johnson & Dbox, James Gibbs, Eris Schuldenfrel
(animation)*

AREA
*Structural area: 90,420 sq. ft.
Plot area: 15,070 sq. ft.*

PROGRAM
*Institution headquarters, exhibition space, art
school residence, educational center, theater,
digital archive, restaurant and bookstore*

This well-known New York-based firm of architects was commissioned to design the new installations for the New York Museum of Art and Technology. This museum is located in the Chelsea district and is set to become the first institution devoted entirely to media art. The intention is also for it to be the biggest institution in the United States for this field of artistic creation. To this end, a revolutionary building was called for that would integrate video and electronics with architecture in a particularly special manner. In short, it would be a complex where the connections between science and art could be explored, using the new technologies.

The complex is designed with different spaces to house exhibition rooms, a students' residence, a study center, multimedia-equipped lecture rooms, a theatre for the new art media, a digital archive, a restaurant, a library, and a bookstore.

The project is based on an apparently simple scheme, formed by a large panel continuously twisting vertically. As it twists, various spaces, intended for distinct uses, are formed. This flexible structure has two parts: first, the spaces intended for production (the workshop) and second, those given over to the presentation of works produced in the workshop (the museum and theater). Similarly, one side is for the long-term residents of the building (students, teaching staff and administrative staff), and the other, for temporary users (visitors to the museum and theater). In spite of this division, if one goes upward through the various levels, the two spatial categories alternate because the route links the two distinct spaces.

The spaces intended for the production of works of art call for a uniform distribution of natural as well as artificial light, while the exhibition spaces each have their own lighting. Thus, the exhibition side will have rooms with a good many light and dark rooms, depending on requirements.

The building's facade is mostly open to view from the outside, thus enabling the passerby to observe the paths taken by residents and visitors, sometimes parallel to and sometimes crossing each other.

Photo © Perrault Pro

New Mariinsky Theatre

St. Petersburg, Russia   2009

ARCHITECT
Dominique Perrault Architecture

CLIENT
Russian Federation Ministry of Culture, Federal Agency for Culture and Film, North-East Directorate for the Construction, Reconstruction, and Restoration of St. Petersburg, Mariinsky Theatre State Academy

PARTNERS
DPA Russie (associate architects); Joseph Clark (consultant); Perrault Projects (architectural engineering); Georeconstructizia-Foundamentproekt (surface engineering)

AREA
Plot area: 150,700 sq. ft.
Built area: 645,835 sq. ft.

VOLUME
17.66 million cu. ft.

COST
230 million euros

PROGRAM
Theatre with 2,000 seats for operas, ballets and symphony concerts; large public patio; stores; restaurants; exhibitions; studios; administration; parking; etc.

This new cultural building has been planned for Russia's second largest city. St. Petersburg. The city's architecture is marked by its baroque and neoclassical religious buildings, with an essentially Italian influence, which have been preserved in perfect condition over the years. The Russian skyline is marked by domes, vaults, and golden steeples, as well as large buildings housing museums, palaces, and leisure centers. The exact site of the new Mariinsky building is in the heart of a complex network of canals and streets, close to the historic first Mariinsky Theatre, beside the Kryukov canal.

The French architects who won the international competition to design the new building wanted to reflect a new structure that spoke of its origins, while opening itself up to the world to be admired. The result was a marriage of history (expressed in the use of glistening gold) and modernity (reflected in a multivolume structure), a union that makes the whole an artistic icon the world will identify with the city of St. Petersburg.

The building consists of a main vestibule, a 2,000-seat auditorium; a smaller 350-seat room; the stage; artists' and technicians' dressing rooms and workshops; rehearsal rooms and studios; storerooms; the administrative department for opera, ballet and concerts, technical spaces and parking; a public restaurant and various stores; and a telescopic bridge connecting this building with the earlier Mariinsky Theatre.

The new theatre is designed as an all-encompassing volume in black marble covered by a translucent glass cupola with glistening gold structure. This external skin emphasizes the volume of the surrounding buildings, and, in the passages inside, this skin engenders open spaces that afford views of the exterior at all times. Inside, the main passage is fully lit with natural light coming through the glass panes of the main structure. The decor of the theatre is typically a combination of red and deep gold, colors which are used on the rows, balconies, walls, and ceilings as if they were all part of a canvas.

In this project, form and function establish a perfect arrangement of technical rationality and flexibility. In the heart of old St. Petersburg, this structural geometry reflects a perfect symbiosis between heritage and modernity.

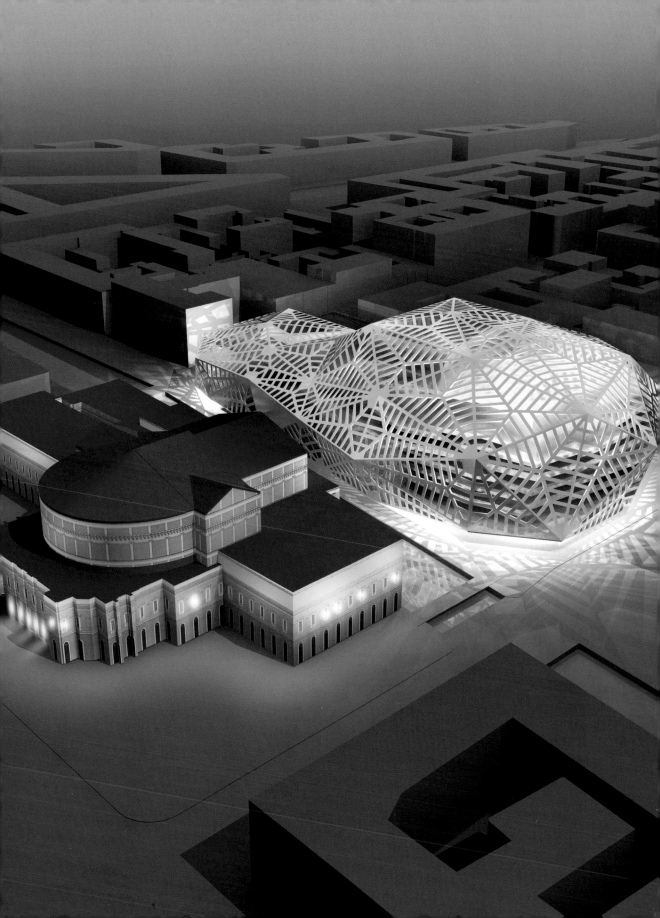

Location plan

The main design of this project consists of a black marble structure covered by a translucent glass cupola integrated by glistening gold linear latticework. The main passage stretches all across the new Mariinsky Theatre and is the antechamber to the rest of the services. The architects wanted to display at all times the marriage between the Russian architectural heritage and the contemporary nature of modern buildings.

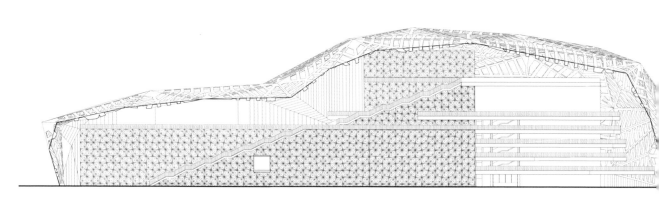

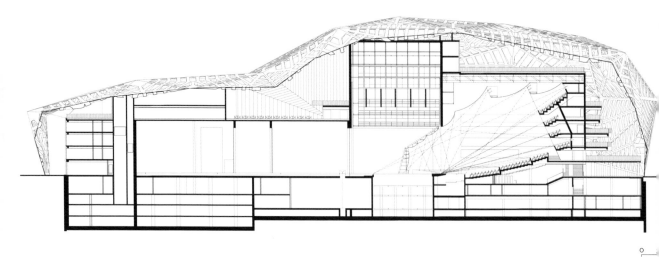

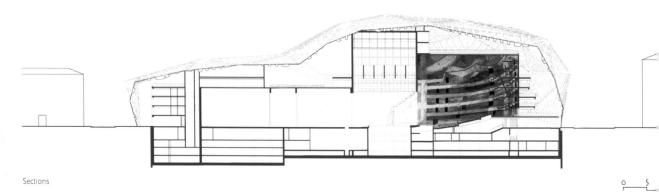

Sections

0   5

Photo © Softroom Archite

Tree House

Mobile, Virtual   1998

ARCHITECT
Softroom Architects

CLIENT
Wallpaper *Magazine, Tyler Brulé*

AREA
161.5 sq. ft.

PROGRAM
Design for a cabin attached to a tree

This group of architects came up with a set of four projects for *Wallpaper* Magazine, and the Tree House is one of them. The client gave free rein to the architects, with the only condition being that they design a tree house. As the commission was to be delivered on paper, the architects took certain liberties as far as the structure scheme and construction were concerned. The project is the result of a thorough study of function and form, an academic exercise that has never been undertaken. In spite of the structural liberties, this type of tree house—with the right resources—can be built today.

The resulting structure is a very light composition that can easily be transported and attached to a large tree trunk. This cabin has minimum impact on nature, easily blending in with it. Its composition consists of rings that support a triangular frame allowing for different spaces. The various spaces are laid out seamlessly and combine elements such

as a picnic table, a bed, a toilet, and various observation platforms. The installation of other elements, such as water pipes, solar panels, and gas bottles makes the unit self-sufficient, incorporating the necessary functions to make it habitable. As well as its simple, quick assembly, a system of cables is also proposed that may be extended to neighboring trees, thereby creating a network of platforms that can be laid out all over the forest.

The use of high-technology computer-assisted design, or CAD, was essential in generating this design and enabled the architects to show even the smallest detail. Thus, all angles, textures, and materials were created to provide a highly realistic picture of the dwelling.

This is a good example of the work of this London-based architecture firm, which specializes in emphasizing the relationship between architecture, the interior, and the natural surroundings.

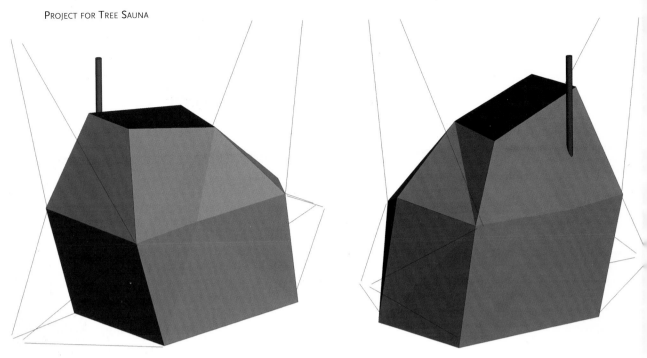

Photo © Ari Bung

Sauna

Pirunsaari Island, Finland   1998

ARCHITECT
Ari Bungers/Lab-arkkitehdit

AREA
130 sq. ft.

VOLUME
1,130 cu. ft.

PROGRAM
House including a sauna built onto a tree

The main objective of this project was to design a house situated among trees that would fulfill the function of a typical Finnish sauna. The result is a total of three structures fulfilling different functions. The unit is situated on an uninhabited island, some 300 miles to the north of Helsinki. The surroundings include mature pine forests, wild berries, and woodland shrubs, all just a few yards from the Baltic Sea. The area's inaccessibility has meant that the splendor and beauty of this favored location has been preserved. It can only be reached by taking a boat and then walking for several miles.

One of the architect's main objectives was to preserve the natural surroundings to the maximum. Therefore, construction of the house in the trees had to cause as little impact as possible on the environment. The most appropriate solution was to hang the structure above the ground, thus creating the sensation that it was floating amidst the tree-populated terrain. Stressed steel cables support the structure at various points and, at the same time, stabilize the construction. The structures used to create this original design are polyhedral shapes that give rise to multiple planes both inside and outside. The main house, which functions as a sauna, is flanked by the other two structures, which are service areas and fulfill the rest of the functions of a typical house. As well as the sauna, the first structure contains the living areas (a dining room and a patio) and the main bedroom. Inside, the space is divided into two levels which are connected by small staircases. Access between the three structures is achieved by bridges that hang from the surrounding trees.

The main construction materials are wood and steel, which form metal rings and extensible tubes and are supported on a timber structure. These materials blend in perfectly with the natural environment, to the extent that they are unnoticeable among the trees. The original shape, structure, and composition make this project perfectly feasible in practice.

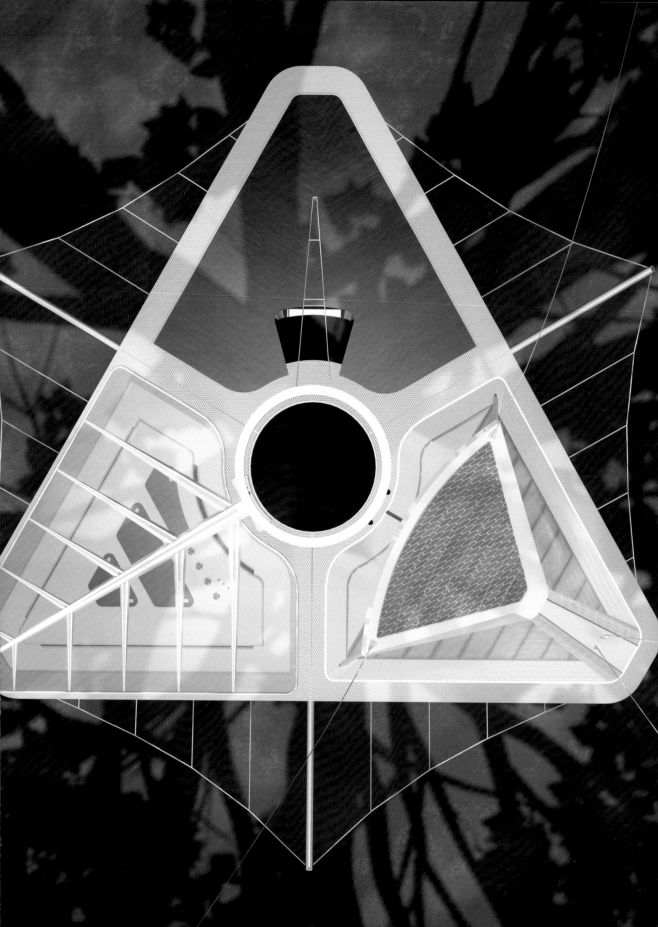